PENGUIN BOOKS

KICK THE TV HABIT!

Steve and Ruth Bennett are the co-authors of the bestselling *365 TV-Free Activities You Can Do with Your Child,* as well as a number of other activity books designed to give parents of kids four years of age and up a jumpstart on creative play.

Steve is a full-time author who has penned more than fifty books on parenting, the environment, business management, and microcomputing. The former president of a technical publishing company, he holds a master's degree in regional studies from Harvard University.

Ruth is a landscape architect and illustrator who has designed public parks and playgrounds in a number of cities in the United States. She holds a master's degree in landscape architecture from the University of Virginia.

The Bennetts live with their two children, Audrey and Noah, in Cambridge, Massachusetts.

STEVE AND RUTH BENNETT

Kick The TV Habit!

A Simple Program
for Changing Your Family's
Television Viewing and
Video Game Habits

PENGUIN BOOKS

PENGUIN BOOKS
Published by the Penguin Group
Penguin Books USA Inc., 375 Hudson Street,
New York, New York 10014, U.S.A.
Penguin Books Ltd, 27 Wrights Lane, London W8 5TZ, England
Penguin Books Australia Ltd, Ringwood, Victoria, Australia
Penguin Books Canada Ltd, 10 Alcorn Avenue,
Toronto, Ontario, Canada M4V 3B2
Penguin Books (N.Z.) Ltd, 182–190 Wairau Road,
Auckland 10, New Zealand

Penguin Books Ltd, Registered Offices:
Harmondsworth, Middlesex, England

First published in Penguin Books 1994

1   3   5   7   9   10   8   6   4   2

Illustrations by Ruth Bennett

Grateful acknowledgment is made for permission to use the following
material:
Children's Programming Worksheet, reprinted with permission from
Advocates for Children & Youth, Inc./Ready at Five.
Adaptation of selections from *TV Breakouts #2: Children and TV:
What Teachers Can Do to Help* and *TV Breakouts #4: Helping Children
Survive Video Games.* By permission of Children's Television Resource
and Education Center.

LIBRARY OF CONGRESS CATALOGING IN PUBLICATION DATA

Bennett, Steven J., 1951–
Kick the TV habit!: a simple program for changing your family's
television viewing and video game habits/ by Steve and Ruth Bennett
p.   cm.
ISBN 0 14 02.4001 2
1. Television and family.   2. Television and children.
3. Television—Psychological aspects.   I. Bennett, Ruth (Ruth
Loetterle)   II. Title.
HQ520.B46   1994
302.23'45—dc20   94–9626

Printed in the United States of America
Set in Adobe Century Expanded
Designed by Kate Nichols

Foreword

by
Peggy Charren

Founder, Action for Children's Television

Why do our children watch so much television? How does TV affect our kids? What can we do to improve the quality of programming and ensure that television meets our children's needs? And how can family and television coexist harmoniously and productively? These are questions I've been exploring for the past twenty-five years, as a concerned parent, the founder of Action for Children's Television, and an advocate for the Children's Television Act.

While the passage of the act was a very important step forward in paving the way for better children's programming, there's still much work to be done in our homes, schools, and communities. As parents, we need to take an active role in curbing how much television our children watch. The best way to accomplish this is to become role models ourselves. We must also speak out and tell the media what kind of programming we seek for our children and be willing to put ourselves forward as advocates for public broadcasting. Just as important, we need to be aware of the challenges posed by new television, video, and computer technology.

This inspiring book empowers you on all these counts—and helps answer some of those big questions about television and your kids. Steve and Ruth Bennett talk *to* you, not *at* you. No sermons, no diatribes, and no pretense of having the "one-and-only" right answer. Instead, they encourage you to choose where you want to be on a spectrum of viewing options. You define the goals that best meet *your* family's style and personalities, and the Bennetts provide the tools and techniques to help you achieve those goals—without making your kids feel deprived or punished.

The Bennetts' approach is based on a TV-reduction partnership that enables kids to learn how to self-regulate their own viewing habits. And to really make the effort worth it for your children, try some of the nifty activity ideas you'll find in the second part of the book. They'll help bring out your child's creative side while enhancing your family relationships as well. (You'll also find it invigorating in our hustle-bustle world to rediscover the simple art of play!)

Sure, it's easy to say "yes" to television when we have to say "no" to so many other things in our children's lives. But by adopting a TV-reduction partnership, you'll take an important step in curbing the influence that television has on your children. You'll also help your kids become "TV-smart," so that when they do watch, they're more likely to choose programs that have the kinds of programming qualities you're seeking for them.

If you want to go beyond your own living room, you can work together with friends and neighbors to ensure that a precious public commodity—the airwaves—is used wisely. The Bennetts offer much practical advice for initiating school-wide and community-wide television-awareness campaigns.

As much as I like the book's easy-to-use format and strong encouragement for parents to provide television alternatives, what attracted me most is the authors' belief that censorship or government regulation of program content is not an answer to the "TV problem." The solution lies in reconsidering the way we use television ourselves and the way we allow the broadcasters to use our airwaves. If we really want to solve the TV problem, we need to change our own TV watching habits and work with others to ensure that broadcasters provide enough good TV choices for our children. And we can accomplish this by sending a strong consumer message to the broadcasting industry.

Finally, I think the timing of this book is terrific—and not only because of the current debate on television violence. With the coming revolution in telecommunications, we're on the threshold of a world in which we may be doing just about everything with our television sets: shopping, banking, relaxing, and learning. So we'd better figure out now how to take control of the technology in our own living rooms so that it best serves our families, today, tomorrow, and well into our children's future.

Acknowledgments

We're deeply indebted to many people for making this book a reality. First, we'd like to thank those who gave us so much of their time and put up with sometimes lengthy interviews:

Dennis Albertson, Beth Brownlow, Laura Bucuzzo, Jerry Carmady, David Considine, Margo Cunningham, Nancy DeSalvo, George Gerbner, Evan Imber-Black, Dawn Jacobs, Sandy Kendrick, Pamela Kennedy, Kathryn Montgomery, Monica Mullins, Gil Noam, Parker Page, Jim Prochaska, Janine Roberts, Marieli Roe, Sally Rogers, Ann Simonton, Dorothy Singer, Robin Templeton, Kathleen Tyner, John Wright, Charlene Hughins Uhl, and Maryanne Wolf.

Special thanks to Diane Levin of Wheelock College for giving us a crash course in key developmental psychology issues; to Parker Page, president of the Children's Television Resource and Education Center, for his review of portions of the manuscript; to Peggy Charren, founder of Action for Children's Television, for inspiring our thoughts about using the political process to bring about change in the media; and to Carleton Kendrick for sharing so much of his clinical work and thoughts with us.

Stacey Miller was instrumental in helping to develop the manuscript and shape the ideas in this book from the onset of the project—once again, we owe you one, Stace. Richard Freierman and Kate White also provided invaluable assistance in developing material and manuscript. Marcy Ketcham helped prepare the manuscript and researched entries for the resource section. Our agents, Lynn Chu and Glen Hartley, did their usual terrific job of packaging our ideas and dealing with the business side of the project. Thanks, team!

Our Viking Penguin team also played a key role in translating our ideas into a finished book. Publisher Kathryn Court believed in and supported our project from the start. Our editor, Nicole Guisto, helped us make important decisions and shepherded the book through the publishing process—thanks, Nicki. And hats off to Kate Nichols, who did a splendid job of designing the book.

Finally, our most important team members, Noah and Audrey Bennett, put up with the usual craziness that goes along with bringing a book over the finish line. We're once again amazed by your patience, and are more grateful than you can imagine for inspiring us to write about kids and television in the first place. This book, as always, is first and foremost for you.

Contents

PART II. Your Family

PART IV. Your Community

SECTION TWO: TV-Free Activities

The Media Consumer's Resource Guide

Introduction

Television. It's been called the one-eyed monster, the plug-in drug, and a host of other epithets. Some experts urge us to throw our television sets out the window; TV poses a terrible threat to the minds of our young people, they say. Others claim that television is one of the most important technologies of this century and will become even more so in the next century (we just need to "fix" the programming a bit). Then there are those in the evolving "media literacy" movement who urge us to become critical viewers: to "decode" and understand the messages found not only in television but in radio, newspapers, video, and all other inputs to our "media society."

Who's right? And what should you, as a parent, do about getting a handle on television? We believe that there are elements of truth in all of the above philosophies. Commercial television—particularly programming aimed at children—is in a horrific state ("a national disgrace," as George Gerbner, dean emeritus of the Annenberg School of Communication, says), and a mountain of evidence strongly suggests it represents a serious hazard to our nation's youth. At the same time, television *could* be a marvelous tool for communicating information, providing quality entertainment, teaching cooperative problem-solving skills, and breaking down stereotypes—*if* broadcasters choose to follow those routes. Finally, it's true that there are ways of watching other than the traditional "sponge" mode, in which you passively absorb the information; you can "engage" or "talk back" to your television set by questioning and challenging what you see—that's what media literacy is all about.

How much television your family watches is a personal decision, and we would be pretentious if we were to prescribe a viewing formula for "good" parents. While some parents report that getting rid of their television was the best thing they ever did—it led to calmer kids, more time together, and an end to battles over how much time to spend watching—others find that some level of viewing is inevitable, and even feel that certain programs are worth watching.

Clearly, there's a wide spectrum of viewing between "ZTV" (zero television) and watching seven-plus hours a day, the national average. In this book, we provide you with tools for changing your position on that spectrum; you decide how much change is appropriate for your family and how fast the adjustment process will take.

Before describing how best to use the book, we want to share our own position on television so that you can evaluate our ideas and the way we've interpreted insights gleaned from extensive interviews with psychologists, psychiatrists, communication experts, teachers, school administrators, and, perhaps most important, parents who have struggled with and finally made peace with their television sets.

We chose to move our family close to the ZTV end of the spectrum, and today our one small television set spends most of its time hibernating in the closet. (A friend jokes that it's too small to be a real TV; he says it's the security monitor from our old office.) We made that decision for ourselves and for our children, aged four and seven at the time of this writing, for a number of reasons.

First, we're deeply concerned about many of the negative messages that so much commercial television conveys: Why should kids who watch cartoons and prime-time action shows be led to believe that malice is the primary motivator of human beings and that conflicts are generally resolved—and often within a half hour—with verbal abuse, physical force, or firepower? Why should children—or anyone else—be exposed to messages about nutrition that fly in the face of all current medical knowledge? How can we expect to create a cohesive society if women and the elderly are often trotted out for the purpose of being victims, and ethnic minorities for the purpose of perpetrating crimes? And how can we expect our teenage children to make responsible decisions about relationships when the characters they see on television so often act impulsively and irresponsibly?

Second, we deplore advertising and programming designed to prey on children's vulnerabilities and exploit their innocence. Kids of all ages need to establish their unique identities, and they're particularly susceptible to the influence of television stereotypes that define the ideal body and the ideal way of navigating through difficult situations—usually in terms that are alien to most of the population.

Third, we believe spending hours watching today's programming is generally a waste of precious time that we could spend interacting with our families, playing, enhancing relationships with loved ones, developing skills, exploring our neighborhoods, or just doing those things that always seem to get pushed aside until tomorrow. Here's the real litmus test: If you were to look back over your life now and total all the hours spent in front of the tube, would you feel you had invested the time wisely?

Now, having said all that, we believe television could be a useful medium for expanding our understanding of the world. And it could truly address the diverse needs of all our communities. The problem is that right now, television is light-years away from reaching its potential.

If we, the television consumers, make enough noise, though, the media producers will listen. After all, the industry has a bottom-line focus, and if its executives perceive enough consumer demand for television programs, video games, movies, and other media that don't resort to violence, stereotyping, and other negative influences, they'll meet it.

But before we can identify what we want from producers, we need to become critical viewers (that's where media-literacy training comes in). And before we can become critical viewers, we need to get unhooked. No one can be media-literate and decode the subtle—and often destructive—messages present in so much media today, and go on to work for positive change, unless he or she uses television voluntarily, rather than out of habit. And that's the whole point of this book.

A Program for Getting Unhooked

In the following pages, you'll find a step-by-step program for changing your television-viewing habits. The program is designed so that you can apply the basic TV-reduction concepts to other sources of concern these days besides television watching, such as video and computer game playing.

Kick the TV Habit! is organized into two sections: (1) "The Program," and (2) "TV-free Activities," a collection of ready-made games and projects you can turn to instead of watching the tube. The first section contains four parts and is based on the model shown in Figure 1.

Part I begins with your child, the center of the model. This part offers summary information and statistics about violence,* nutrition, stereotyping, and other problem areas associated with television today. We also provide questions designed to stimulate further thinking about how television affects your child's language, behavior, and self-esteem. With a better understanding of your child's TV viewing, you can proceed to the second circle in the model, your family.

fig. 1

In Part II, we discuss a step-by-step process for developing a customized program for cutting back viewing hours to a daily goal of your own choosing. Whether that goal is two hours, one hour, or zero hours, you'll find proven tips and techniques from parents who have "been there," as well as insights from mental health professionals and teachers who have worked with many children and families. This part includes an introduction to media literacy and explains where you can obtain further information on teaching your child critical-viewing skills. It culminates with ideas for extending your TV-reduction program to video and computer games.

The third ring of our model moves out from the family and takes

---

* When we use the term *violence* we use the definition offered by George Gerbner, Michael Morgan, and Nancy Signorielli in "Television Violence Profile No. 16: The Turning Point. From Research to Action": "Violence is a social relationship. People hurt or kill to force (or deter) unwanted behavior, to dominate, to terrorize. Symbolic violence is literally a 'show of force.' It demonstrates power: who can get away with what against whom."

you to your child's school, where you can help to organize and launch a "television-awareness campaign." As explained in Part III, such a campaign involves a "TV turndown" designed to show people that it is possible to live without TV, or with less television, for a specified amount of time. It's also designed to focus attention on how schools can teach children to become critical viewers, defuse television's most negative effects, and get the most out of whatever positive programming exists today and may come down the pike tomorrow.

In the fourth and final ring of the model shown in Figure 1, we consider the positive action all of us can take as a community. The chapters in Part IV explain how to apply a national strategy for changing children's television (developed by the Washington, DC-based Center for Media Education) on a community-wide basis. By forcing broadcasters to comply with the Children's Television Act, you'll ultimately be working toward the creation of programming that meets the needs of all of our children. You can then use the same organizing principles to open a dialogue with producers of other media and to demonstrate that a ready marketplace exists for non-exploitive and non-damaging products that truly represent alternatives to today's sad offerings.

In addition to the chapters covering the program, in Section Two you'll find more than 100 activities that can be done with children of all ages as alternatives to the tube. Consider them as jumping-off points for TV-free action—they form the foundation for as many variations and additional ideas as you can dream up. And other than safety concerns, there are no right or wrong ways to do them. Ideas range from innovative indoor sports to making the most of your local library. We've also included plenty of ways to spend quality time with your child even when you're too tired to put much energy into game-playing or when you're on a tight budget.

Finally, the Media Consumer's Resource Guide provides thumbnail descriptions of media watchdog groups, media literacy organizations, and media research organizations. It also names important books and videos on television issues and provides a listing of television lockout devices. The Appendices offer a sample weekly viewing diary you can use to keep track of viewing time, TV "time slips" for monitoring viewing time during your TV-reduction program, and a sample checklist for evaluating local television stations' efforts to provide the kind of children's programming mandated by law.

The Philosophy Behind Our Approach

We recognize that changing screen-viewing behaviors—watching television and playing video and computer games—can be a trying task for everyone involved. That's why we urge parents to approach TV-reduction efforts with empathy and understanding, rather than simply mandating change through parental edict. At some point, you may have to say, "Because I'm the parent, and I have to make choices for us." But that should be a last line of defense. By exploring and acknowledging your child's feelings and then trying to fill whatever void he or she experiences when you cut back on the tube, you'll have the best chance of changing your child's viewing patterns with minimal pain.

You'll also boost your chances of success if you involve your child in creating alternative activities, and if you allow for negotiation. Curbing television, like so many parenting efforts, can be a win-win situation—with a little forethought and planning, you can let your child make choices within a framework you create.

In addition, it's critical to constantly stress that you're not "taking away" but are giving your child back control over his or her mind and time. At first your child might not believe it, but eventually he or she will greatly appreciate the benefits of watching less TV and spending more time pursuing other interests. We've yet to talk to a parent whose child hasn't accommodated to less TV and felt better in some way for it.

Finally, we firmly believe that your own viewing patterns and style have a tremendous impact on your child. So unless you "watch like you talk," you won't be a very credible role model, and you can't expect much out of your kids in the way of compliance. On the other hand, if your children see the strides that you and your spouse or other adults in the house have made in reducing your own viewing, they may be inspired to do the same. As we say in Chapter 20, "The Tube Stops Here!"

A Word of Advice: Be Patient and Be Flexible

The same issues may come up again and again until your child adjusts to your new viewing rules. You'll have to deal with "unsanctioned" viewing, as well as other people in your life who may not share your concerns about television and video games, such as baby-sitters, relatives, and the parents of friends. Patience and flexibility will keep you from going crazy and will keep your TV-reduction program on course.

Over time, you may also have to alter your program to meet your child's changing social needs. For example, when our son was in first grade, he once complained that he couldn't play with some of the older kids during recess because he didn't know the characters of a popular science-fiction show. So we taped a few episodes and watched them together. This gave him enough information about the characters' moves and maneuvers to beam down with the best of his buddies. And we were pleased to find that this approach didn't stimulate a desire to watch the program on a regular basis.

The point is, challenges await all families when they attempt to control television viewing. Look at them as opportunities to devise clever solutions that don't compromise your position, rather than as potential showstoppers that can send you reeling back to square one. Remember, when the going gets tough, the tough get creative!

Whether you use our book to ultimately give your TV set the old heave-ho or to cut back your family's viewing hours to a level that feels right for you, we know you'll greatly enjoy the time you gain. And what else do we have on this earth but time? Time with our children, time to contemplate our lives, time to watch the last rays of a sunset disappearing into the night sky.

Steve and Ruth Bennett
Cambridge, Massachusetts
January 1994

Kick the TV Habit!

SECTION ONE

The
Program

Your Child 1

Stick 'em Up

Bringing Violence into Our Family Rooms

" . . . I have an eight-year-old and a five-year-old child. They've never seen any of the shows I've ever produced. They shouldn't be watching them. They're not allowed to watch Saturday-morning cartoons." So said Dick Wolf, producer of *Law and Order* and *Miami Vice*, in the August 22, 1992, edition of *TV Guide*. Mr. Wolf has made a wise choice, given what we know about the effects of violence in the media.

Know the Facts about TV and Violence

- "The scientific debate is over," said Dr. Leonard Eron at a forum on television viewing and violence sponsored by Mediascope. Dr. Eron based his assertion on an analysis of more than 200 studies published in 1990. "All types of aggressive behavior, including illegal behaviors and criminal violence, demonstrated highly significant effects associated with exposure to television violence," he commented.

- Based on his studies dating back to the 1960s, Dr. Eron also concluded that the more frequently subjects watched television at age 8, the more serious were the crimes for which they were convicted by age 30.

- The National Association for the Education of Young Children (NAEYC) cites three important effects of violent television on children: (1) desensitization to the pain of others, (2) increased fears of the world around them, and (3) increased aggressiveness.

- During children's daytime programming, violent acts appear 20 to 25 times an hour.

- Writing in the *Journal of the Writers Guild of America West,* David S. Barry noted that by the end of elementary school the average child will have seen 8,000 murders and 100,000 acts of violence, and by the end of the teenage years that figure will have doubled. Others suggest that the number of murders watched may exceed 25,000 by the end of high school.

- According to Dr. George Gerbner, a leading researcher on violence and dean emeritus of the Annenberg School of Communication, "Humankind may have had more bloodthirsty eras, but none as filled with images of violence as the present. We are awash in a tide of violent representations the likes of which the world has never seen." (*New York Newsday* editorial)

Issues to Think About . . . Questions to Ask

▶ How does your child respond to viewing violent acts on television? What is your reaction to their response? Does their response surprise, upset, or concern you? If so, how?

▶ Is your child sometimes frightened by what he or she sees on television? What sorts of images or characters are most upsetting? What images have scared your child in the past but no longer have the same effect today? Do you think repeated exposure to these images has been a factor?

▶ What kinds of TV shows does your child favor? How do you feel about his or her choices? How do you convey your concerns about certain shows? What is your child's response to these concerns?

▶ What role does violence play in your child's favorite shows? How do you think the programs enter into your child's solitary play and play with friends?

Dubious Distinction

The United States is now the most violent country in the industrial world, leading in homicides, rapes, and assaults. (*NAEYC Position Statement on Violence in the Lives of Children*)

Children See, Children Do

Imitating TV Characters Rather than Playing for Real

Ah, to be a child and have the freedom to indulge in pure fantasy play. At least that's the way it used to be. Today many experts believe that television has undermined the way children play, largely because of the availability of action toys like those associated with shows such as *The Mighty Morphin Power Rangers* and *Teenage Mutant Ninja Turtles*. Kids imitate the cartoon characters they see on television, essentially substituting reruns of specific episodes for creative play. Imitation may be the best form of flattery, but when it comes to play, it's a poor substitute for the real thing.

Know the Facts about TV Toys and Play

- In 1984 the FCC deregulated children's television, legalizing the marketing of toys associated with TV shows. By December 1985 all of the ten bestselling toys were based on TV show characters or had appeared on a "special" program, and 80 percent of television programming was produced by toy companies. So was born the program-length commercial.

- In 1985 the sale of war toys in the United States surpassed $1 billion. That represents a 400 percent increase since the deregulation of children's television. The sale of all children's books did not reach $1 billion until 1990.

- When the first Teenage Mutant Ninja Turtle movie premiered in March of 1990, more than 1,000 Turtle products were marketed, including dozens of toys. Turtle toys have been on the top ten bestselling toy lists ever since, even though many teachers have had to ban them from their classrooms because of the problems they create when children bring them to school.

- According to Drs. Diane Levin and Nancy Carlsson-Paige, authors of *Who's Calling the Shots?* (see resource section), "Many of the TV shows and toys marketed with them are highly divided by gender, so that they promote very narrow, sex-role stereotyped play for boys (fighting and strength) and for girls (helplessness and prettiness). The highly realistic toys channel children into mimicking what they see on TV, including violence, and discourage the kind of imaginative and creative play vital for healthy development and learning."

Issues to Think About . . . Questions to Ask

▶ What kinds of toys does your child have? How does your child play with them? Do the toys get used in a variety of ways? Do some toys promote more diverse play than others? Which do and which don't?

▶ What kinds of play does your child enjoy? Does the content of his or her play come from TV programs or from direct experiences your child has had?

▶ How has your child's play developed and changed over time? Can you think of examples of your child using his or her imagination or being creative in ways that seemed special and unique? When? What happened in this play?

▶ What role do you take in your child's play? Are there times when you have learned something from watching your child play or when you have helped your child develop a new aspect of his or her play or come up with a new way to use a toy? When was it? And how did you do it?

One Potato, Couch Potato

The Fattening of America's Youth

Potatoes have been given a bad rap: They're actually not fattening at all until you glob on the butter and sour cream. But the couch potato isn't so fortunate. A number of researchers have found disturbing links between television viewing and obesity, due to the sedentary nature of watching TV and the exposure to high-calorie/high-fat food commercials. No wonder many experts recommend going light on the butter—and the tube!

Know the Facts about TV and Fitness

- The American Academy of Pediatrics warns that "obesity and elevated cholesterol levels are two of the most prevalent nutritional diseases," and TV viewing has been associated with both.

- Researchers at the University of California found that children who watch more than two hours of TV per day have two times the normal risk of high cholesterol than their peers who watched less; four hours of daily television was correlated with four times the risk. They also concluded that excessive television viewing is even more predictive of high cholesterol than a family history of heart disease or cholesterol problems.

- According to the Center for Science in the Public Interest, adults who watch at least three hours of TV daily are more than twice as likely to be obese as those who watch one hour or less.

- Dr. Robert Klesges of Memphis State University discovered that when children watch television, they slip into a semiconscious state in which their metabolic levels are closer to those of sleep than of wakefulness. Among other things, this means that they burn fewer calories. He also found the effect to be more pronounced in children who were already overweight.

- The Center for Science in the Public Interest counted a whopping *223* food ads aired during four hours of cartoons one Saturday morning (the three major networks plus Fox). Of these ads, only 9 promoted foods with acceptable levels of fat or sugar.

Issues to Think About . . . Questions to Ask

▶ What new food products does your child request? Where does he or she learn about these new foods? How do you feel about the products, and how do you feel about the way you handle requests for those items you don't want your child to have?

▶ What does your child know about good nutrition? What has TV taught him or her about the foods that growing children need? How does this information affect his or her requests for various food products?

▶ What role does TV play in your child's daily routine? How receptive is your child to your suggestions for alternatives to television?

▶ How often does your child choose to watch TV over playing outside? How do you feel about this, and what would you like to change?

Seven Years Down the Tube!

In 1989 the average child in the U.S. spent more time watching TV than performing any activity except sleeping. By the time American teenagers of today turn seventy, they will have watched seven years of TV. That's seven sedentary years!

At War with Words

Robbing Our Children of Time to Read

Experts unanimously agree that reading is the key to long-term academic success. They also agree that TV watching directly competes with reading. Cut back on TV viewing hours, they say, and you will increase your child's attention span, foster curiosity, and encourage exploration through books—and very possibly turn your child into a better student.

Know the Facts about TV and Reading

- "Television is one of the single greatest impediments to full literacy in society today," says Dr. Maryanne Wolf, a developmental psycholinguist and neuropsychologist at Tufts University. "It, along with video games, represents the most insidious challenge to the development of imagination among children."

- According to the American Academy of Pediatrics, the average preschool child watches 28 hours of TV a week, the average elementary school student watches 25 hours a week, and the average high school student watches 28 hours a week (approximately six times the amount of time spent doing homework). Some informal surveys by high school teachers reveal a staggering 40 to 45 hours of TV viewing per week.

- The percentage of 13-year-old students watching three or more hours of TV each day jumped from 55 to 70 from 1982 to

1990, and for 17-year-olds, from 31 to 50 percent from 1978 to 1990, according to a 1992 Educational Testing Service report.

- In 1990, $1 billion was spent on children's books; eight times that was spent on children's war toys, most of which are linked to TV cartoons.

- The Reading Report Card for the Nation and the States, issued by the National Center for Education Statistics, found that among students at grade four, lower average reading proficiency was noted for those who reported four or more hours of television viewing each night. For eighth graders, reading proficiency dropped after three hours of watching, and twelfth graders showed a significant decrease in proficiency after just *one* hour.

Issues to Think About . . . Questions to Ask

▶ Does your child spend more time watching TV or going to school? Doing homework? Reading? Engaging in a hobby?

▶ How does your child spend his or her free time? How are decisions about spending free time made? How do you feel about your child's use of free time?

▶ How have your child's preferences for free time changed as he or she has gotten older? What have been the major causes for those changes?

▶ How does your child respond to your suggestions for reading or other non-television activities? What activity does your child most often see you engaged in during your free time?

A Commercial Break

Creating Consumers: The Next Generation

Flip on Saturday-morning cartoons, and you'll turn your television into an electronic toy store and junk food kiosk. While the passage of the Children's Television Act has helped to reduce the number of ads network stations can broadcast, the number of commercials is still staggering. And the concern is not just for kids; as the Center for the Study of Commercialism sums it up, "Rampant commercialism is transforming Americans from *citizens* into *consumers*. We are raised in a torrent of slick, seductive advertising that beseeches us to buy, buy, buy."

Know the Facts about TV and Commercialism

- A committee of the American Academy of Pediatrics found that "the main goal of children's television is to sell products to children."

- According to *Broadcasting and Cable* magazine, children's programs attracted $800 million in television advertising in 1993—that's out of about $150 billion spent on media advertising in the United States.

- Children are exposed to at least an hour of television ads for every five hours of programming they watch; the average American child sees 20,000 ads a year.

- The American Academy of Pediatrics notes that "commercials for meat, milk products, bread, and juice make up only 4 percent of the food ads shown during 'children's viewing time.' " Yet according to *Adbuster's Quarterly,* teenagers see 100,000 alcohol ads before they reach drinking age!

14

Issues to Think About . . . Questions to Ask

▶ How does your child decide what to put on his or her "wish list"? What role does each of these play in influencing your child's birthday or holiday gift list the most: Peers? Their own interests? Family? Television ads?

▶ Have you ever sensed that your child's attitudes or behavior were influenced by a certain item advertised on television? What did your child say to convey his or her feelings? How did you respond?

▶ Has your child ever been disappointed by the smaller, slower, less glamorous, more breakable reality of toys that appear larger, faster, more glamorous, and more powerful when shown in TV ads? How did he or she react? What did you do?

▶ How does your child convey desires for toys and other products to you? How do you respond? In what ways do you feel your response working or not working? What would you like to change if you could?

▶ Do you think advertisements convince your child that happiness, popularity, and self-confidence come from material things? Has your ability or willingness to provide products advertised on TV even become a measure of your love for and interest in your child?

Look But Don't Touch

A University of Massachusetts study conducted on behalf of UNPLUG (see resource section) showed that "Channel One"—a 12-minute, advertiser-funded news program delivered via satellite to 8 million students by nearly 12,000 participating schools—is disproportionately adopted by schools in high-poverty communities. The study, which included 17,344 schools, determined that "Channel One" is found in 60 percent of schools that spend less than $2,600 a year per student, while only 10 percent of schools that spend more than $6,000 a year opt for the program. "'Channel One' is more often shown to the students who are probably least able to afford to buy all the products they see advertised," the study concluded. "It requires no stretch of the imagination to suggest that this in turn may enhance their alienation and frustration."

Images That Hurt

Perpetuating Racial, Ethnic, Gender, and Other Stereotypes

If a visitor from another planet were to study Earth on the basis of television broadcasts, he or she (or it) would get a very skewed view of who's important, who's disposable, and who, apparently, can do what to whom. "Even noble attempts to redress ethnic, gender and other under-representations often fail," says Dr. Gil Noam of Harvard University, "because simply substituting one or another group for mainstream, white figures doesn't achieve anything; television fails to depict the continuous, hard work that goes into overcoming fears of differences."

Know the Facts about TV and Stereotypes

- "In prime time, about 5 percent of all the characters and 10 percent of the major characters are involved in killing. 'Bad' men and women, and Hispanic and lower-class characters do most of the killing. Older men and women, women of color, and lower-class characters pay the highest relative price for their acts," concludes a 1993 study by George Gerbner, Michael Morgan, and Nancy Signorielli.

- In a June 1993 study presented to the Screen Actors Guild and the American Federation of Radio and Television Artists, Dr. Gerbner found that people of color make up only 13 percent of the program casts during prime time and less than 5 percent of the casts in children's television. Specifically:

  - African-Americans are less than 11 percent of prime-time and 3 percent of children's television casts.
  - Latino/Hispanics account for 1 percent of prime time and less than 0.5 percent of children's television.

- Americans of Asian/Pacific origin and Native Americans are virtually absent from the screen.
- According to Dr. Gerbner's research group, people with physical handicaps appear in about 1.5 percent of prime-time shows.

- Researchers Nancy Carlsson-Paige and Diane Levin note that "many children's television programs promote suspicion, intolerance, and even violence against those who are different. Racial and ethnic stereotypes are common. Often, 'bad guys' have characteristics that are different from the 'good guys' who represent mainstream white U.S. Society. 'Bad guys' are often from foreign countries and speak with foreign-sounding accents. Many are dehumanized altogether—with computer-simulated voices, masks that disguise their faces, and maimed or robot-like bodies. Good characters fight violently against the bad; they can hurt and easily hate these characters whose humanity is rarely shown."

- According to Ann J. Simonton, the director of Media Watch (see resource section) who for the past fifteen years has been tracking how women are portrayed in the media, "Women are still being characterized pedominantly as victims of violent crimes. Worse, in many shows, the plot lines glamorize or promote women as 'asking for abuse.' When women are shown in a 'power' role, they're usually cast as vengeful, deceitful, and manipulative people doomed to failure of one kind or another."

Issues to Think About . . . Questions to Ask

▶ Do you ever see your child imitating behaviors, gestures, or verbal expressions of TV characters that are hurtful or demeaning to people different from him- or herself?

▶ How does your child react to people noticeably different from him- or herself? With curiosity? Indifference? Fear? Distrust?

▶ What do you feel television teaches your child about those different from him- or herself? How does this compare with what you would like him or her to think?

▶ Has your child's play been defined by gender stereotypes? Can your daughter be a doctor as well as a nurse? Can she be the boss? Can your son take care of the baby? How would your children repond to your efforts to expand their play possibilities?

Do You Think I'm Sexy?

Misinforming Our Children About Love, Sexuality, and Relationships

Television has forever altered the way most children learn about family relationship issues, values, and problems. Whereas older children once relied on family and trusted community figures for information on marriage, love, sexuality, and commitment, they now learn about life from situation comedies, crime shows, soap operas, and whatever other offerings network executives dish up and local station managers serve.

Know the Facts about TV and Sexuality

- The American Psychological Association (APA) estimates that American teenagers are exposed to 14,000 sexual references and innuendos per year on television. Of these, only 150 deal with responsibility, abstinence, or birth control.

- The APA also notes that implied sexual activity on television occurs "most often between unmarried couples with little commitment to one another."

- Drs. Dennis Lowry and David Towles call TV's presentation of sexual behavior a "disinformation campaign" where few women who use no contraception get pregnant and almost no one has a sexually transmitted disease.

- In a study by A. Tan, "High school girls who saw fifteen commercials that emphasized sex appeal and/or physical attractiveness were more likely than girls who saw a set of neutral commercials to say that beauty characteristics were important for them to feel good about themselves and to be popular with men."

Issues to Think About . . . Questions to Ask

▶ What does your child learn from TV about love, marriage, sex, family, and relationships? How does this compare with what you'd like him or her to learn?

▶ What types of relationships are portrayed in your child's favorite shows? How do you feel about the level of commitment, responsibility, and caring that the characters have for one another?

▶ What do you think your child's selection of shows is based on? Do you believe the portrayal of impulsive, "spontaneous" relationships enhances the appeal of the program to your child?

▶ What would you like to change about the relationships portrayed in your child's favorite television shows? How do you think these changes would be received by your child?

▶ What messages about sexuality and self-esteem appear to affect your child most? Have you noticed your child trying to transform him- or herself into somebody who is slimmer, taller, or more glamorous because of what people on television look like?

Lo Cal, Please—Kiddie Portion

A survey of 494 middle-class schoolgirls in San Francisco revealed that more than 50 percent of the students considered themselves overweight; in reality, only 15 percent were medically overweight. Of the ten-year-olds surveyed, *81 percent said they were on diets!*

"Vidiotics"

Desensitizing Our Children Through Violent Video Games

Few consumer items have generated as much controversy as video games. Whereas most of us grew up with television, video games are more recent inventions to which we've had little—if any—exposure. We don't have a great deal of scientific data directly linking these games with violent behavior, but common sense tells us that games based on killing and savage themes can't be good for our children.

Know the Facts about Video-Game Playing

*   According to Japanese researchers, children who play computer games longer and more frequently than others tend to be more aggressive, competitive, and energetic.

*   According to Dr. Eugene Provenzo, author of *Video Kids,* "Of the 47 top-rated games in a Nintendo Power poll in 1991, only 7 did not have violence as their major theme."

*   Dr. Diane Levin notes that the typical violent video-game player wins points largely by killing opponents. No points are awarded for problem solving, mediation, or cooperative behaviors.

*   Americans spent $200 million on home video games in 1978. By 1981 the market had grown to $1 billion. Today it represents a $4 billion-plus market.

*   Dr. Terri Toles found that less than 10 percent of the parents of video-game players knew the content of those games.

Issues to Think About . . . Questions to Ask

▶ What role do video games play in your child's life? What other kinds of play does your child enjoy? How do you think video games influence your child's play?

▶ What do you think video games teach your child about the nature of war, fighting and weapons, good and evil, and how conflicts and problems get solved?

▶ What do you know about the content of the video games your child plays? How do you feel about it? What role does violence play in your child's video games?

▶ How do you and your child select new video games? How does the content of the games enter into the decision-making process?

Gee, Aren't You Just *Dying* to Buy It for Your Child?

In a preview of Mortal Kombat II (MK II), *GamePro* magazine said, "You can expect MK II to be as gory as its predecessor. Reptile's Fatality Move, for example, involves his removing his hood to reveal his lizard head. His tongue then darts across to the stunned opponent's head, which is ripped off and slurped into Reptile's mouth with a stomach-rubbing 'Mmmm.' Other Fatalities have Johnny Cage pulling his adversary's torso off and throwing it down; Jax smashing his opponent's skull with a single, thunderous hand clap; and Baraka (the other-worldly alien) extending swords from his arms (à la the T1000 from *Terminator 2*) and chopping off heads."

Your Family

First, a Word from Our Sponsor

Understanding the Prerequisites for Success

Now that you know some facts about TV viewing and its effects on your children's behavior, you're probably eager to begin developing a program for changing your family's TV-viewing habits and style. But before diving in, you ought to sort out a few key issues regarding the participation of your children, support from your spouse or other adults in the household, and your own level of commitment. This preliminary step is essential if your program is going to be a long-term success.

Who's on the Planning Committee?

There are two ways to develop and implement your program:

1. gain the active participation of your children, or

2. impose one by edict.

We strongly recommend that you opt for the first approach, since the sooner you gain your children's cooperation, the more quickly they'll learn to self-regulate their TV watching and be more critical viewers when they do watch "sanctioned" shows. You can either inform your child about the program as you plan it and involve him or her in the development, or you can wait until all the pieces are in place and have an official kickoff (Chapter 19). In any case, there are plenty of opportunities to involve your child in the planning process.

A Family Matter

Later on in this book we'll discuss the importance of being a good role model—your children's viewing behavior is in part based on your own. Are you willing to set an example and live without some, or all, of your favorite shows? How about your spouse or other adults living in the house? Or relatives who visit frequently? Remember, the responsibility starts with you!

Make It Real!

While your screen-time-reduction program won't demand forty hours a week to administer, it will require some up-front time and commitment. If you approach it tentatively or halfheartedly, your kids will pick up on your ambivalence and reflect it in their own willingness to get with the program. Choose a time when you can treat your TV-reduction program as a worthy cause, and make sure that you're available for "co-viewing," family activities, and lots of good old-fashioned talk.

Action Steps!

1. Get support from other adult household members.

2. Pick a reasonable date to begin the program.

3. Start practicing: Flex your off-button finger!

The Ubiquitous Appliance

According to the Electronic Industries Association, 92.1 million (out of 93.8 million) American households own television sets. Of these, 35 percent own one set, 41 percent own two, and 24 percent own three or more. According to *Adbusters Quarterly*, more American homes have TV sets than plumbing!

Moments of Truth

Tracking Your Family's Viewing Time

How much television does your family *really* watch? Even families that assume they have a handle on screen time are often surprised at the weekly tally. If you're looking to reduce television watching through gradual weaning, rather than pulling the plug and instituting a zero-TV policy, then it's especially important to track how much time you and your family members spend sitting in front of the tube. You can then establish realistic goals and a timetable for achieving them (see Chapters 11 and 12).

A simple way to chart your family's viewing hours is to maintain a one-week log (we've provided one on page 118). Whether you use the log or write notes on the back of a napkin, here are some record-keeping tips:

DO:

✔ Fill out the log each night, rather than waiting until the end of the week and depending on your memory.

✔ Try to include your family in the tracking process; this is a good way to encourage participation in your program. It's also essential if you have latchkey kids with unrestricted access to television sets.

✔ Post "TV-tracking reminders" on the family bulletin board, refrigerator, and near each television set in your home.

DON'T:

✘ Choose a hectic time to keep the log, such as the holiday season, or a time when abnormal viewing may take place, like sick days or while a house guest is visiting.

✘ Fret about maintaining perfect records; your program won't fall apart if you miss a show or two.

✘ Play "I spy." If you're doing the monitoring rather than your kids, be honest about your intended use of the information.

The Art of Successful Screen Tracking

- If you have more than one television set, place a pad and pencil by each one. Consolidate the information into one "master" log for easy tabulation.

- Try to set up a regular daily meeting time, perhaps before bedtime, to sit down with your family and fill out the log.

- Encourage older kids to help younger siblings with timekeeping—this is a great way to get your children involved.

- Consider making a game of it; see if family members can guess how much time they spend watching TV, then announce the results at the end of the week.

Action Steps!

1. Pick a starting date for filling out the viewing log, and make sure that the time to be monitored represents a typical week.

2. Photocopy the form on page 118.

3. Start logging!

Who Knows Where the Time Goes?

According to *TV Guide*, TV viewing takes up 30 percent of America's spare time, followed by socializing, reading, do-it-yourself projects, and shopping.

It's About Time

Establishing Viewing Goals for Your Family

Now that you've totaled up the hours your family spends in front of the television, it's time to figure out what you'd like that number to be in the future. Here are some guidelines for developing viewing goals.

To Watch or Not to Watch

Are you hoping to achieve a state of zero-TV? Many families have found that getting rid of their television sets offers tremendous benefits, such as freeing up time, calming down their kids, reducing the effects of commercialism, and ridding the house of "noxious" influences.

Except for those families starting off with very young children, however, zero television is probably unrealistic. Kids who have had a steady diet of television watching for several years or more may have a very difficult time adjusting to life without the tube; television has come to shape their world in many subtle ways. Also, you may feel that certain programs are enriching and worthwhile, and provide quality entertainment. So most likely you'll be looking to reduce viewing to an acceptable number of "approved" programs each day (see below). What's acceptable will vary from family to family, although the American Academy of Pediatrics recommends *no more than one to two hours of daily TV viewing*.

Play the Ratings Game

The math for a TV-reduction program is simple: If your child is spending four hours a day in front of the tube and you want to cut back to one, then three have to be eliminated. To decide which ones will go, take a look at all the shows listed in your viewing log, then organize them into three categories:

A. *Thumbs-Up.* Shows that you feel are educational, reinforce your values, or provide quality entertainment.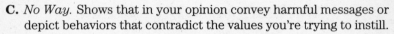

B. *Negotiable.* Shows that don't strike you as particularly harmful or offensive, but don't contribute anything to your child's knowledge of the world or sense of how to act in it.

C. *No Way.* Shows that in your opinion convey harmful messages or depict behaviors that contradict the values you're trying to instill.

Now write down an ideal week made up of the "A" programs, noting and totaling their viewing lengths. Congratulations, you now have a set of weekly viewing goals! In the next chapter, you'll learn how to decide on a timetable for getting from where you are today to your ideal viewing level. (By the way, if you have more "A" programs than you need to fill up a week's worth of viewing, that's great—you can give your children choices, which will be a tremendous boost in making your program a success.)

Action Steps!

1. Watch the shows your children watch; you can't rate them unless you know their content.

2. Rate the shows and decide on an ideal viewing week.

3. Formulate an explanation of your show ratings. When you present the program rules and viewing alternatives, your children will benefit from learning your criteria; hopefully, they'll even be able to apply them on their own in the future.

Advice from the Top

Why does Henry Becton, general manager and presidentof WGBH-TV, Boston's Public Television affiliate, ban television—even "educational television"—from his home on weekdays? "Our children are in their prime homework years," Becton told the *Boston Herald* after testifying before the Massachusetts Committee on Education. He believes that "their time during the week should be spent on homework and reading." He admits that he makes the occasional exception. For instance, his son watches *NOVA*—but only on videotape.

Pace Yourself

Deciding on a Time Frame for Your Program

At this point you know how much time your family is spending in front of the tube and how much time you'd like them to be spending in the future. You also know the landscape of an ideal viewing week. But how long will it take to achieve your ultimate goal: a week, a month, a year? Two approaches you can take are:

1. The Direct-to-Goal Route

Perhaps your children are watching an average of five hours of television per day, and your goal calls for one hour. Immediately lopping off four hours can be fairly dramatic, bordering on "cold turkey," but you may decide this is the easiest way to reach your family's viewing goal. (By the way, you may hear of parents who advocate an initial "detox"—no TV for a few months—followed by a gradual reintroduction of television. We can find no reason for this approach, and believe it will only cause undue strife.) When taking the direct-to-goal route:

- Begin the viewing reduction when you can be available for activities and special occasions; again, your empathy, encouragement, and involvement will be key to getting your kids over the initial hump.

- Be prepared to acknowledge any resentment and anger you may encounter. Rehearse what you'll say (such as "I know you're not happy about this, but . . ."; see Chapter 19 for suggestions).

2. The One-Show-at-a-Time Phaseout

The least-wrenching way to achieve your viewing goals is through gradual weaning: say, eliminating one show a week, or one show every two weeks. Of course, you can eliminate two shows a week just as well; just remember that the ideal is to cut back *gently*. You've already drawn up a list of "*shows to go*" (the "C" category shows discussed on page 29), as well as programs that can be used for negotiating purposes (the "B" category shows). Now you need to lay out a timetable for cutting back to the desired viewing time. Use the following chart to create your own "TV Phase-out Guide":

Day	Shows to Watch	Shows to Eliminate

Action Steps!

1. Discuss with other adults living in the household an appropriate time frame for achieving your viewing goals.

2. Write down the major milestones on a calendar: 50 percent reduction, 75 percent reduction, etc. Younger kids might relate more to "only three shows per day," "down to two shows per day," and so on. You can also tie these important achievements to celebrations and acknowledgments for good work (see Chapter 14).

Rules to Watch By

Determining How Your TV-Reduction Program Will Work

You now know what you're trying to achieve, and how long it will take to get there. The next step is to establish the specific game rules for watching. It's important to establish these rules up front, so that you eliminate ambiguities and the potential for confusion. The following questions are meant to help you tailor your program to your child's personality and how much television he or she has watched in the past.

Questions to Consider Before Establishing Viewing Rules

▶ Will your child watch the same amount of television each day, or will there be different limits set for weekdays, weekends, and holidays?

▶ Will the TV-reduction program be put aside during sick days?

▶ Will your child be allowed to accumulate any unused hours in a "TV bank"—and make withdrawals against viewing hours "saved"?

Deciding What to Watch

▶ Will you let your child "cherry-pick" a certain number of shows each week from an approved list (the "A" or "B" category programs described on page 29)?

▶ Will you and your child scan the television listings each week and together decide which shows to watch?

▶ How will you handle requests for viewing special shows?

What's Your Watching Style?

▶ Will your child be allowed to watch television unaccompanied, or will you or another adult always "chaperon" him or her?

▶ Will you videotape and review all programs before your child may watch them? If so, will you "zap" the commercials when you play the tape for your child?

▶ Will you make it a policy to have the whole family watch television shows together and discuss the issues raised?

Other Issues

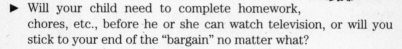

▶ How often will you recognize your child (and other family members) for sticking to the program, and what kind of acknowledgments will you offer (see the next chapter for suggestions)?

▶ Will you make it a policy to have only one television set on at a given time?

▶ Will your child need to complete homework, chores, etc., before he or she can watch television, or will you stick to your end of the "bargain" no matter what?

Action Steps!

1. Make a list of program elements using your answers to the above questions as a starting point.

2. Commit your program to writing, so that you can later make and distribute copies to your family members, baby-sitters, and all others who will need them.

Rooms with a View

In a study reported in 1992 by the National Coalition on Television Violence, 47 percent of the children polled had a TV set in their own room. Of these, only 50 percent said that their parents had viewing rules.

Way to Go!

Creating a Recognition System for Your Program

Cutting back on TV watching can be a difficult process, so your family may need lots of positive feedback and reinforcement for sticking to the rules and making the program a success. Recognition shouldn't be confused with rewards, though. As Dr. Diane Levin explains, "Long-lasting change comes when your child feels some sense of responsibility and inner satisfaction, rather than working towards the goal for an external reason." She recommends devising ways of acknowledging an accomplishment that help the child reflect on and validate what he or she has achieved. For example, when certain milestones are reached:

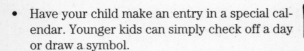

- Have your child make an entry in a special calendar. Younger kids can simply check off a day or draw a symbol.

- Make a pin, medallion, trophy, or certificate with your child to acknowledge special accomplishments.

- Have your child choose—and perhaps even help shop for and prepare—his or her favorite meal or dessert.

- Have your child write about the accomplishment for a family gazette or newsletter.

- Enact a ritual designed for the TV-reduction effort, such as playing a special game with the whole family, having you or your spouse give a special family "toast" at dinner, or giving one another a special cheer before bedtime.

Tips for Recognizing Your Child's Achievements

- Always use the recognitions as an opportunity to make your child feel he or she has done something important. At the end of the first day, for example, talk about how great it is that your child is participating in this very worthwhile effort.

- Acknowledge your child each day for the first two weeks or so. At the end of the first and second weeks, hold a special celebration. Be prepared to work in acknowledgments whenever an infusion of pride and praise is needed to sustain the effort.

- Don't seek perfection before recognizing your child's efforts; you'll get closer to perfection if your child is encouraged to be proud of whatever he or she has achieved in the program so far.

- Don't underestimate the power of your words of praise. Younger kids especially need to hear how well they've done and how proud of themselves they should be.

Action Steps!

1. Brainstorm a list of acknowledgments that will make your child feel good about participating in the program.

2. Decide on major milestone recognitions—say, successful cutback by 25 percent or 50 percent—and plan special celebrations, dinners, etc.

3. Gather the materials you need so that recognitions can be created as they're called for.

Scout's Honor

Monitoring Screen Time in Your House

To be effective, your TV-reduction program will need to be monitored for adherence to the game rules you developed in Chapter 13. It's important to decide ahead of time how compliance will be measured and enforced. While you want to make it clear that you're serious about the program, your children shouldn't feel they're under surveillance from the "TV Viewing Police Squad."

The Low-Tech/No-Tech Approach

Provide everyone with TV time slips (photocopy the models on page 119). Ideally, your children will monitor themselves and stick with the game rules on their own. This is more likely to happen if they can negotiate (within certain boundaries) about what they watch and if they perceive the benefits of cutting back on their viewing hours. Plan on giving the honor system a boost by:

- Making it easy for kids to keep track of their TV watching with TV time slips.

- Commending your children when they do a good job of tracking themselves.

- Planning to start off on the basis of trust—a position of strength for both of you—and with an understanding that if lapses occur, you'll re-explain the purpose and benefits of the TV-reduction program (see Chapter 19) and try again.

- Play along yourself. Let your children check your TV time slip— you're all in this together!

High Tech: Fighting Fire with Fire

A variety of gizmos are available for controlling and monitoring TV viewing. They range from simple gadgets that allow the tube to be operated only by means of a key switch, to electronic devices that let parents indicate when the television will operate for different members of the family (see resource section). Before purchasing a technological fix for a nontechnological problem, however, consider the following:

- TV-control devices should be regarded as last-ditch alternatives, not first-line options. A control device is no substitute for understanding your child's need to watch TV and working hard to include him or her in the planning process.

- When you rely on control devices from the get-go, you're communicating a powerful message—"We don't trust you"—that can be demeaning as well as counterproductive.

Action Steps!

1. Make up enough TV time slips so you can place them by each set, along with a copy of the week's approved shows.

2. Devise acknowledgments that will be given for using the time slips and making the honor system work.

Stealth Viewing

Today's whiz kids can often outsmart today's technology. One father told his latchkey children that he'd ordered a locking switch, and their days of endless viewing would soon be over. The clever kids intercepted the package when it arrived, carefully opened it, took the key to a local hardware store and had it duplicated, then resealed the package. The parents only caught on weeks later, when they realized that the set was hot all the time!

Fun and Games 16

Filling the "Days of Darkness"

The hardest part of turning off the television—but probably the most critical—is figuring out what your kids are going to do without the "plug-in drug" and what *you're* going to do without the electronic baby-sitter. How can you creatively fill the hours formerly spent in front of the tube—without spending a fortune or driving yourself crazy? By devising great TV-free activities!

Jump-Start Your Imagination

Sit back for a moment and imagine a world without pressures in which you can fully enjoy being with your kids. Think in terms of arts and crafts, indoor and outdoor sports, learning games, day trips, read-alouds, and other activities. Now pick one idea. What kind of preparation do you need? What would be the best time to do it? How would you begin? How long would it last? How could you modify it? Jot down your answers.

Congratulations! You've just created your first TV-free activity. The more you do this exercise, the easier it will be for you to come up with new games and projects. Try to think of activities designed to be done by your child alone or with friends, and for times when you can't participate yourself. (Also, see Section Two, which offers many ready-to-play activity ideas you can tailor to your children's ages and interests.)

Hints for Activity Brainstorming

Here are some things to keep in mind when creating TV-free activities:

- Look for common household objects that can be turned into arts and crafts projects, science experiments, etc.

- Focus on areas that will be of special interest to your child; you're the best expert on his or her interests.

- The less complicated the better, and the more you'll be willing to let your child modify the activity.

- Think in terms of flexibility—the more easily the activity can be modified, the better the chances you can tailor it to your child's interests.

- Don't worry about whether you have what it takes to come up with creative activity ideas—anyone who used to be a kid can remember fun things to do!

Action Steps!

1. Think about activities you did as a child. How can you recreate them?

2. Ask friends for their favorite activities; you might even establish an informal activity bank or network.

3. Ask older relatives what they did to entertain themselves when they were children. They're bound to suggest good TV-free activities.

The Best of TV-Free Times

Getting the Most Out of TV-Free Play

Perhaps you've brainstormed some TV-free activities of your own, or maybe you've selected a few "ready-to-play" activities from Section Two of this book. Either way, we suggest that you think about the fine art of play before moving into the action phase of your TV-reduction program. Remember that what kids want more than anything else in the world is your focused time. And they have a marvelous, built-in "presence detector"; they know when you're really focused on an activity with them and when your mind is somewhere else, thinking about paying bills, resolving work issues, and the like. Also, if you're fully engaged in the play, your child is likely to learn how to sustain the activity on his or her own over time. Here's a list of things to think about to make your activities a critical success.

Tips for Playing

DO:

✔ Remember that the more experience children have with appropriate and satisfying non-TV activities, the more skill they'll develop at inventing their own. This ability will likely be greatly satisfying to them.

✔ Offer choices; making decisions about what to do with time is a key goal of your TV-reduction program.

✔ Be open-minded. If family members have a better idea than what you had in mind, or they want to change the goal of a project midstream—great! Other than safety, the only rule should be that there aren't any rules.

✔ Be patient. If your child's play has become imitative because of heavy exposure to television and "single-purpose toys" associated with TV shows, he or she may need a hand in relearning how to play in creative and imaginative ways. To help your child go beyond mimicking TV scripts, encourage activities that draw on his or her direct experience, such as playing school, performing skits and role playing. If your child is attached to violent-action figures, devise projects that involve putting the toys into peaceful scenarios. You can further tame and humanize the action figures by helping your child to make houses, clothes, vehicles, and other nonviolent accoutrements.

✔ Use the activities as opportunities to observe and cherish your child; doing so will sustain your interest and enhance the fun during repetitive play.

DON'T:

✘ Try to do activities when you're rushed or hassled; you'll just frustrate your child if the idea is to finish the game or project as fast as you can.

✘ Focus on competitive aspects of an activity. If a "winner" is called for, de-emphasize the importance of winning by praising all family members for putting forth their best efforts or topping their previous scores.

✘ Worry about large blocks of time. You don't have to supplant five hours of television watching with five hours of activities. Make what time you have available focused time, and strategically schedule activities so they cut across what would otherwise be viewing time.

Action Steps!

1. Look at your own schedule for time you can devote to doing TV-free activities. See what you can juggle, especially in the beginning of the program.

2. Think about developing special "anytime/low-energy" activities you can do during hectic times.

3. Practice playing. Once you get into it, it's not hard to be a kid again!

Pre-Launch Considerations

Learning from Others' Experience

Before you officially start your program, browse through the following general suggestions gleaned from the experiences of people around the country.

- Be realistic about backsliding; change isn't always a linear process, and you might get to your goal by following a zigzag course. Patience will win the day!

- Keep your TV in its place. Don't make it an extra guest at the dinner table; spend dinner time talking, joking, and sharing the trials and tribulations of the day.

- Move the television set out of the main play or family get-together area, so that it's not a centerpiece or "electronic hearth." If you've invested in a "mega-screen monster," fashion a set of curtains or a slipcover that must be opened or removed in order to watch TV.

- Don't allow your kids to "channel-surf," even among shows on your "approved list." Remember, there's a big difference between "watching a specific television show" and "watching television." You and your child should negotiate for watching certain programs—not for the right to become a zombie for a specific amount of time each night.

- Tape shows as often as possible, and zap the commercials.

- Don't get on a public soapbox about your program. Other parents may infer that you're judging them, and they may unconsciously pass that discomfort on to their own children. If friends or acquaintances act surprised about your TV-viewing rules, treat the issue matter-of-factly, saying, "Yes, we've cut back here" or "Yes, we've made some choices for our family," then move on to the next topic of conversation.

- Try to anticipate problems and formulate a plan. If you've gotten rid of your TV set and your school occasionally makes television-based assignments, either plan to seek alternate assignments for your child (which may put him or her in the awkward situation of being "different") or rent or borrow a television for the occasion.

- If your television breaks down, take your time getting it fixed—you'll be amazed at how the indisputable fact that "it's in the repair shop" or "it costs a fortune to fix" will end all sorts of battles and confrontations. At the least, it will make subsequent cutting back easier. Who knows—you just might want to leave your set in the shop for an extended vacation!

Action Steps!

1. Review your TV-reduction program; are you comfortable with all the details?

2. Review your explanations to all the people who will be involved. Perhaps rehearse a few sample dialogues and key phrases (see next chapter).

3. Review your start date. Is it the best time (or the least-worst time) to start the program?

4. Take a deep breath and begin!

The TV-Reduction Partnership

Discussing the Program with Your Children

Perhaps you've included your children in planning much of the TV-reduction program, so they are familiar with the details. If not, at this point you'll need to begin discussing the new viewing rules. Your message and your delivery style will greatly affect how well your children receive the program.

The Partnership Approach

Throughout this book, we've stressed the importance of working with your children, honoring their feelings, and giving them a say in what they can watch (based on your list of approved shows; see Chapter 11)—in short, treating them like partners whenever possible. Here are some key points to convey to them now:

- "Watching less TV will help everyone in our family. We'll have more time together and more opportunities for fun."

- "Change is often difficult, so this may not be easy for any of us. But we're in this together, and we can help each other."

- "Let's talk a lot about how we're feeling—and try to help each other."

Suggestions for Discussing Your TV-Reduction Program

Your children's response will depend on many factors, not the least of which is how much television they're accustomed to watching. Even so, consider a few "universals" when you break the news:

DO:

✔ Pick a time when you can adequately deal with your children's response. You don't want to be forced to cut short the discussion because you or your kids have to be someplace else.

✔ Focus on the positive elements of the program, such as how much the quality of life will improve and how much easier it will be to find time to do fun things.

✔ In households with more than one adult, use phrases like "*We* feel that . . .," "*We're* concerned that . . .," "*We* hope that . . ." This will remind your children that the grown-ups stand together on the TV issue.

DON'T:

✘ Speak in "punitive terms," such as "From now on you're going to watch only . . ."

✘ Get into arguments or prolonged debates about *why* you're launching the TV-reduction program; they're a sure road to frustration. State your reasons for pursuing the new rules, and answer questions about *how* the program works. And hold your ground if you're challenged.

✘ Broach the subject during particularly busy times. While there may not be a perfect time to explain the new rules, don't let the program become a means for venting other frustrations.

Action Steps!

1. Select a date for explaining the program to your children, but be flexible enough to postpone the talk if the family's mood isn't conducive at that time.

2. Discuss with your spouse or partner the best ways to present the program.

3. Anticipate your children's feelings.

The Tube Stops Here

Modifying Your Own TV-Watching Behavior

How often do you turn on the television set for your viewing pleasure? Do you automatically flip it on while you cook, clean, or exercise, so that it becomes a kind of background noise?

Your own viewing behavior communicates an important message to your children. If your TV is always on in the background, you're telling them that it's important life-support technology; if you treat your television set as just another appliance, like the stove or vacuum cleaner, your children will assume it has a purely utilitarian function.

Here are some viewing tips for you and other adults in the household:

DO:

✔ Make sure the TV set is always off while you're doing at-home work (paying bills, making dinner, etc.). Remember the message you're communicating to your kids.

✔ Make sure watching television requires some effort. Try moving your set to a less prominent spot—perhaps a remote corner, cabinet, or closet—and drag it out only for news or something you really want to see.

✔ Let your kids see you reading books, magazines, and newspapers instead of watching television.

✔ If you watch news, a movie, or a favorite program, decide in advance on a turn-on and turn-off time. Then stick to it so that you don't leave the television set on out of habit.

✔ Make time to do something you've been wishing you had time for: read a certain book, bake bread, or write a letter to a relative. Then tell your family about what you did with your "liberated" time and how pleased you were to have done it.

DON'T:

✘ Rearrange your schedule to watch a television show. That makes the show seem much more important than it probably is.

✘ Channel-surf. If you don't want to watch anything that's on, shut off the television.

✘ Watch TV while exercising. Save the electricity for something worthwhile.

✘ Grant yourself "permission" to stay up late to watch a television show.

Action Steps!

1. Announce to your kids that you've decided to watch less television so that the family will have more quality time together.

2. Report on your own progress to your family members.

3. Watch Like You Talk!

The Hidden Full-Time Job

The average American family watches television a little more than seven hours per day. That's roughly:

50 hours per week
220 hours per month
2,600 hours per year
Or:
9 solid days per month
110 days per year
1,100 days per decade

What could you do with all that time?

All for One

Convincing Spouses and Partners to Get with the Program

Are there adults in your household who can't overcome their dependency on television? If so, there's good news from Dr. James Prochaska, a clinical and health psychologist at the University of Rhode Island and co-author of *Changing for Good* (see resource section). Dr. Prochaska has developed a comprehensive method for changing chronic behaviors such as smoking, overeating, and drinking, and you can use his method to help adults kick their TV habits. It entails recognizing the phases people go through when attempting to break an "over-learned" behavior, then offering support to help them achieve success.

Phase 1: Pre-Contemplation. Here, the person is not yet seriously intending to change the behavior. He or she may be unaware of the negative consequences of continuing the behavior, or may believe that the pros of maintaining it outweigh the cons.

What can you do: Talk about the problems associated with commercial television today (cite the facts listed in Part I of this book). Explain how all adults in the household need to be role models, the benefits to the children, the opportunities to enhance family relationships, etc.

Phase 2: Contemplation. There is serious thought about changing the behavior, but the perceived pros and cons tend to be equal. This causes ambivalence, which can keep the person stuck or turn him or her into "chronic contemplators."

What you can do: Begin a dialogue about how the person feels, acknowledging what may be lost by cutting back on TV viewing, and then discussing other possibilities. If, for example, he or she sees the tube as the only way to wind down from the day and relax, pose alternatives for "decompressing" that don't involve television.

Phase 3: Preparation. The person is committed to altering the behavior, and believes that the pros of changing clearly outweigh the cons. The person is ready to work on a plan for change.

What you can do: Jointly develop a strategy for implementing TV-free alternatives. If TV fulfills a need for "space," then discuss how your spouse or other adults can have a special "no-demands" half-hour period just before dinner, anywhere but in front of the TV. Set realistic goals; perhaps start with one day a week, and expand gradually.

Phase 4: Action. This is the actual implementation of the plan. It's also the time of greatest temptation for relapse.

What you can do: Be supportive, offer lots of empathy, and commend the person for being such a good model for the kids.

Phase 5: Maintenance. Temptation to lapse falls off. The longer the person continues in maintenance, the less the risk of relapse occurring.

What you can do: Be understanding; occasional returns to the old pattern don't signal a complete relapse. Gently coach your spouse or partner to get back on track, and work to develop new TV alternatives.

Action Steps!

1. Learn the hard facts about the negative effects of television watching and share them with other adults in your home.

2. Start thinking about TV substitutes that make sense for adults.

3. Stick it out. Kicking the TV habit is one thing that really does get easier as time passes!

Thanks for Your Support

Enlisting Help from Grandparents and Baby-sitters

Let's say you've gotten your own viewing under control, you and other adults are acting as good role models, and your child has bought into the TV-cutback idea. What will happen when your child visits grandparents or when he or she is under the supervision of baby-sitters and opportunities for "breaking the rules" arise?

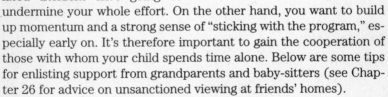

On the one hand, it's important to remember that an isolated incident isn't going to undermine your whole effort. On the other hand, you want to build up momentum and a strong sense of "sticking with the program," especially early on. It's therefore important to gain the cooperation of those with whom your child spends time alone. Below are some tips for enlisting support from grandparents and baby-sitters (see Chapter 26 for advice on unsanctioned viewing at friends' homes).

Grandparents

When children visit grandparents, they often make a beeline for the television set once parents have left for errands and outings. Sometimes grandparents see turning on the television set as the easiest (and least expensive) way to fill time. And kids often regard grandparents as "pushovers" for allowing them to watch what they want. Counter this by:

- Explaining to grandparents what you're trying to accomplish and making your concerns about television understood.

- Describing how your program works and emphasizing that you expect your child to comply with the rules at all times.

- Most important, offering grandparents a list of activities geared toward older people's needs—games that don't require top physical fitness or 20/20 eyesight, for instance. *Be sure to provide whatever materials are required!*

Baby-sitters

Whether your child is going to the baby-sitter's home or the baby-sitter is coming to yours, you are temporarily relinquishing your authority to enforce your television-viewing policies. Here's how to make sure your baby-sitter serves as a boost, rather than a hindrance, to your TV-reduction program:

- When hiring new baby-sitters (or before deciding to use former sitters again), make your television-watching rules clear—and part of the conditions of their ongoing employment with you.

- Present the baby-sitter with a list of specific activities to choose from, and have all the materials handy for doing them. The idea is to eliminate any excuses for turning to the TV for entertainment.

Action Steps!

1. Commit your TV-reduction program to a simple-to-read, one-page document that can be photocopied and handed out to others.

2. Devise and practice delivering a three-minute verbal explanation of your program.

3. Create and fill a portable "anytime activities" bag to take to grandparents', baby-sitters', and other caregivers' homes.

Tradition, Tradition, Tradition!

Creating Non-TV Family Rituals

Every family has its own rituals, whether they involve a weekly visit to a favorite restaurant, birthdays and other celebrations, reading a story before bedtime, or playing games on a given weeknight.

Perhaps one of your family rituals involves sitting down in front of the TV set to watch certain shows. You'll probably want to think about changing that ritual to reinforce your television-reduction efforts. As Dr. Evan Imber-Black, professor of psychiatry and director of family and group studies at the Albert Einstein College of Medicine and co-author of *Rituals for Our Times: Celebrating, Healing, and Changing Our Lives and Our Relationships* (see resource section), points out, "If your nightly ritual is watching TV together, you'll get some benefits from being in the same room together. But it also means that people aren't connecting in an effective and verbal way."

At the same time, rituals need to be treated delicately. They're a "protected time and space. . . . They help us mark the rhythms of our lives and express who we are," says Dr. Janine Roberts, professor of family therapy in the school and counseling psychology program at the University of Massachusetts, Amherst, and co-author of *Rituals for Our Times*. "You don't want to destroy the good feelings that come from sharing time together. Rather, you want to transfer those feelings to rituals that don't necessarily involve television."

Creating TV-Free Family Rituals

Drs. Imber-Black and Roberts suggest that you keep the following in mind when trying to change a family ritual:

1. Plan ahead. Involve all family members in planning what kinds of things you will be doing during the new ritual (for instance, game playing on Tuesday night, or having a special meal and

drawing activity ideas out of a hat on Thursday night). If you simply impose a new ritual in place of the old TV-based one, your children will feel a "double whammy"—the loss of the old ritual, and the resentment of having a new one foisted upon them.

2. Ask everyone in the family to make a list of things he or she would like to do as a family during the special ritual time. As Dr. Roberts points out, "The process of creating the new ritual is as important as the ritual itself; the planning process is a time to make connections with various family members."

3. Discuss the suggestions and decide which ones you would like to try. If you typically watch a show together on Tuesday evening, try out the new ritual on Wednesday. Then, when you find a routine everyone likes, switch the activity to Tuesdays and phase out the TV.

4. Schedule the new ritual for a regular time and place, preferably in a room without a television.

5. Stay flexible! Rituals must change as family members grow and change, or else the rituals become empty.

Action Steps!

1. Announce ahead of time that you're seeking suggestions for new, non-TV-based rituals.

2. Conduct a special planning night or dinner.

3. Propose a (flexible!) schedule for phasing out TV-watching family rituals and substituting new ones.

4. Launch the new ritual with enthusiasm and excitement!

What's So Great About Everyone Sitting Around and Watching the News?

According to *Adbusters Quarterly*, every minute of a TV newscast has about 160 spoken words. The average half-hour newscast runs for 22 minutes; that means it gives you little more than half a page of an average newspaper.

"TV Was"

Understanding Television
WithdrAwal Syndrome

You won't find the term *Television WithdrAwal Syndrome* in a medical dictionary—yet. But at the beginning of your TV-reduction program, your child may in fact experience a period of unhappiness, discontent, or outright anger over not being able to watch certain shows. According to some parents, the "grumpies" can last a month or two. While it's important to remain firm during this difficult period, it's equally important to feel empathetic toward your child. And to feel that empathy, you need to understand the loss your child perceives. Sometimes you must do some clever detective work to figure out what your child gained from a particular show, while at other times the benefits will be obvious.

TV: What's in It for Your Child?

Family therapist Carleton Kendrick describes a few of the common payoffs children get from television watching:

A Means of Empowerment. When a child says, "I like that super-hero because he beats up better than anyone else," he's probably saying that watching the superhero makes him feel powerful himself. "That says a lot about the child's sense of self-esteem and understanding of conflict resolution," says Kendrick.

A Few Good Friends. For some children, television represents a stable and dependable group of friends. "For security, it's unmatched," Kendrick comments. "Once your kids hear the show's theme song, they're home-free. The TV 'friends' are predictable and they don't talk back. When you cut off the program, you may be unwittingly undermining some of your child's sense of security in a tumultuous world."

Role Models. Children turn to television figures—from cartoon superheroes to soap opera and action show stars—for advice on how to get along in the world. Young children, for instance, will often say, "So and so (on television) says, 'You should never do this.'" By eliminating shows featuring these characters (even if you agree with the messages and advice they give), you may be shutting off what your child perceives to be an important information spigot.

"I Want to Be You." "Television makes it easy for children to live vicariously through other people's actions, seductions, and relationships," says Kendrick. Preadolescent girls are particularly susceptible to this lure, as they tend to identify with soap opera and other appealing figures. "Having to be stuck with 'who you are' can be quite shocking," he warns.

Visions of a Perfect Universe. Television distorts reality: Good generally triumphs over evil, bad guys get what's coming to them, an abundant supply of law enforcement people are there to avenge wrongs, family and interpersonal disputes tend to end in harmony, rich people are happy and don't work, and so on. What a great escape from the real world!

Can you identify the hidden payoffs television offers your child?

Action Steps!

1. Tape the programs you've cut out of your child's weekly viewing, paying particular attention to the characters and typical plots.

2. Talk with your child about what he or she liked about the shows and now misses.

3. Discuss how *together* you can help fill the voids.

The "Nerd" Factor

Helping Your Child "Be Different"

If your child doesn't know the characters or plots of a popular cartoon, soap opera, or sitcom because the show isn't on your approved list, will he or she feel like a "nerd"?

Some kids never experience the problem, while others express anger and frustration about being unable to chitchat with their peers about the "in" TV shows. Fortunately, most parents report that the feeling of alienation passes fairly quickly.

Understand the "Passkey" Concept

Odds are, your child will learn about the characters of popular shows from other kids in the neighborhood or school. That exposure will often be enough to give him or her "passkeys"—general ideas about what particular characters do and how they act. Once a child has the passkeys, he or she can participate in almost any discussion about the program.

- If your child insists that he or she can't keep up with friends' discussions of a certain show, watch a couple of episodes together. That will often provide the necessary passkeys and put your child back in the "loop."

What to Say When Passkeys Don't Suffice

If your child craves more than peripheral knowledge of a show, you need to convey your understanding of the desire while remaining firm:

- Acknowledge the need and the hurt; if you imply that your child is silly for caring about something like a TV program, you instantly close off the communication channel and guarantee ongoing resentment.

- "Put it straight," family therapist Carleton Kendrick advises. "Say, 'I know you really want to see this, but we have certain values in this family that we apply to magazines, the language that people in our house use, and what people here say to each other. The same applies to television shows.'"

- "Tell your children how smart, creative, and 'cool' they are," Kendrick also says, "and that they'll still be smart, creative, and cool if they can't annotate the past episode of a popular soap or sitcom. If you've been conveying those things all along, you've got a whole lifetime up to the show to bank on—I'd roll the dice and stack that up against any sitcom any day!"

Action Steps!

1. Be observant during carpooling, play days, and other gatherings of friends for signs of how your child is coping with the TV-reduction program.

2. Make sure that you keep up the praise and reinforcement of your child's personality, behavior, and accomplishments while he or she accommodates to the new viewing rules.

3. Help your child craft an explanation for friends of your new viewing rules. It should stress that neither your viewing habits nor those in his or her friends' households are "right," but rather represent choices every family makes.

When the Cat's Away...

Dealing with Unsanctioned Viewing

Your child will inevitably bump into opportunities to watch "unapproved" programs at friends' homes where there are no viewing restrictions. Grandparents or baby-sitters who don't want to disappoint kids may also allow them to watch rather than fight (refer to Chapter 21). What can—and should—you do when "illegal" viewing takes place?

It's All in Your Head

Your attitudes and expectations regarding unsanctioned viewing will largely determine how much of a problem it is for your household, and how serious a threat it is to your TV-reduction program. Here are some suggestions:

- Be realistic. You can't control every moment of your child's life, nor can you be there to deflect every negative influence. Part of your goal is to help your child self-regulate and make the kinds of choices you'd like him or her to make.

- Relax. Even if you know that your child is watching unsanctioned programs (or TV at all, if you're creating a TV-free household), isolated viewing incidents will not derail your program.

- Don't make your child feel guilty or let the issue provoke a confrontation; that might just make the forbidden fruit all the more appealing. Take it in stride, and it will be less of a problem.

- Think twice before asking parents of friends to respect your viewing rules when your child is at their homes—the issue can be quite explosive and may hurt your child's friendships, especially if the friends' parents interpret your request as a judgment about them.

Seize the Opportunity

One way to make unsanctioned viewing less of a problem is to view it as a potentially positive experience. Here are a few suggestions:

- Encourage your child to be honest about what he or she watched, rather than threatening your child with punishment. Use the unapproved TV watching as an opportunity to apply critical-viewing and message-"decoding" skills (see Chapter 28).

- Discuss the messages and images in the shows your child saw, with an eye toward reinforcing the viewing rules you've set for your family.

- If yours is a TV-free household, consider unsanctioned viewing as one means of satisfying your child's curiosity about the tube; the minimal exposure won't create cravings for more. Pamela Kennedy, a parent educator and early-childhood consultant who raised three children TV-free, actually welcomed unsanctioned viewing. "It showed them what they were missing," she says with a chuckle, "and they quickly realized that it wasn't much!"

Action Steps!

1. Explain that different households have different viewing rules, and that no one's rules are "better" than anyone else's.

2. Learn to inquire about your child's TV viewing when away from home without judging or implying a lack of trust.

3. Encourage your child to exercise his or her best judgment when given the opportunity to watch TV out of the house.

For the Next Round

Evaluating and Refining Your Program

Earlier, you probably selected a date by which you hoped to achieve your TV-reduction goals. When that date arrives, you should take a look at a number of areas, and not just whether you've gotten from three hours per evening to one hour. Most likely you'll want to build on what you learned and achieved, so the next round will be even more satisfying and successful.

Quality of Life

Ask yourself and your family members the following:

- Is the quality of life for your family improving?
- Is anyone still experiencing Television WithdrAwal Syndrome?
- What are the good aspects of the TV-reduction program?
- What are the problem areas?
- Is it getting easier to stick with the program, or does the adjustment still feel painful?
- Has anyone come up with any great ideas about how to spend time away from the television?

If some family members find the program distressing, then perhaps you need to:

- Slow down the pace of change—maybe your goals were too aggressive.
- Work harder to devise more alternatives.
- Further discuss what people miss about shows they're no longer watching.

- Adjust the program rules so that they're easier to follow or so they seem fairer or more palatable.

- Have family members offer more praise for sticking to the program or acknowledge progress more frequently.

Documenting What Went Right

Find out what people in your household found most beneficial about the TV-reduction program. Hold a roundtable discussion in which each person offers one answer to each question.

1. What one thing did you like best about cutting back on TV?

2. What were you able to accomplish with your free time that you otherwise wouldn't have gotten done?

3. What one lesson have you learned?

4. Is there anything you're able to concentrate on or enjoy more now that you're watching less TV?

Feedback: Take It Seriously

Throughout this book, we've talked about the importance of getting your children involved in planning your program. Your kids' ongoing feedback is critical if you hope to extend the program into the future and make it an accepted part of your family's life. Solicit your children's opinions about:

- New activities they'd like to do.

- New family traditions/new family night activities.

- What to do during sick days, snow days, or holidays to resist the temptation to turn on the television.

Action Steps!

1. Set aside a "feedback-and-evaluation night," perhaps with a special snack or treat.

2. Have an older child act as the official record keeper or scribe, writing comments in a notebook.

3. Summarize what you've learned and any changes you've decided to make in the program.

The Media-Wise Family

Developing Critical-Viewing Skills

Perhaps at this point you've reduced the amount of television watching in your household to a more comfortable level. You now have an opportunity to take an important step in helping your child understand and decode the messages contained in whatever shows are on your "approved" list. That's where "media literacy," or critical viewing, comes into the picture: Media literacy helps put TV under the magnifying glass to explain the messages of advertising, as well as the subtle—and not so subtle—themes in children's and adults' television programs. We strongly recommend contacting one of the media literacy organizations listed in the resource section of this book; many provide inexpensive instructional materials for use at home by parents and in school by educators.

Media Lit 101

"The basic idea behind media literacy is to move beyond passivity in order to 'engage' the media," says Elizabeth Thoman, the executive director of the Center for Media Literacy (see resource section). "The umbrella concept is that you're smarter than your TV. We are constantly interacting with what we see, hear, and read based on our age, gender, education, life experience, etc. That's how you and your kids can react differently to the same television show." Thoman stresses the following: (1) Viewers need to know that *all* media are constructed. Someone picked one image over another; even the news is assembled from many potential images, and we never get to see what was left out. (2) Each type of media follows its own formulas. When you understand the formulas, you can more easily separate fact from fiction, such as real news from re-enactments. (3) All media are businesses with commercial interests. That means almost everything we see and hear is subject to being influenced by what will make the most money. (4) All media contain a point of view, because of the preceding. As a result, some people and ideas are presented as being more important than others. And there's the rub: If, for instance, most of the people who get killed are women, minorities, and the elderly, the message is plain—these people don't count.

Try It Yourself

Videotape some of the shows you've approved for watching (*don't* zap the commercials). View the recordings and ask yourself the following kinds of questions. Then do the same with your children.

- How are conflicts resolved—with cooperative effort or force?

- Is violence "clean" and easy for those who use it?

- Who are the heroes, who are the victims? Do they tend to be men or women? Of what race? What age?

- What types of people are shown to be smart, industrious, and successful? What types are portrayed as stupid, lazy, or incompetent?

- How do rich people get rich? Do they work?

- What attracts people to one another?

- What promises of happiness and personal well-being do commercials convey?

- What's the connection between the products advertised and the content of the program?

Do this kind of questioning often enough, and you and your kids will begin seeing your favorite shows—even educational programs and the news—in a new light!

Action Steps!

1. Start thinking about the messages you see in the newspaper, on television, and in movies, video games, and other media.

2. Write or call one of the media literacy organizations listed in the resource section and order parent-training materials.

3. Prepare questions about issues that you can discuss with your kids.

4. Engage the media!

As the Joystick Turns

Extending Your Viewing Program
to Video Games

For many parents, video games are more troubling than television shows. Most reward points for destroying enemies, some contain brutally violent actions, and others convey sexist and racist messages. Video games are also more difficult to control, because there are fewer satisfying alternatives to violent offerings.

Many parents are unaware of the content of the games their kids are playing. In part, that's because the games get progressively difficult, and the uninitiated don't have the playing skills needed to get to the "good stuff," where they can be rewarded for eviscerating an opponent or assaulting a college coed.

Assuming you can find nonviolent alternatives, what can you do with your investment in video game hardware (which your child will be loath to relinquish)? Here are some recommendations from the Children's Television Resource and Education Center (C-TREC— see resource section; adapted with permission from C-TREC's *TV Breakout #4: Helping Children Survive Video Games*):

- *Limit Playing Time.* An hour or so on school days.

- *Alternate Games.* Help your children discover and try out a range of video game software. Regularly substitute more educational games for the purely violent action-adventure types.

- *Play with Your Kids.* They will enjoy teaching you the nuances of the games and you will have a chance to gain a better understanding of their content. Choose games you can enjoy playing with your kids, just as families played board games together in the pre-video game days.

- *Provide Guidance.* Don't let your young children pick super-violent movies at the video store. Treat video games the same way. Shop with your children and help them make selections. Read the game description on the package and check for a rating sticker. If you're still unsure about the content, rent it. Many video stores stock video games as well.

To this we add:

- Learn the content of electronic game magazines that your child may purchase on the stand or subscribe to. As Carleton Kendrick puts it, many tend to be "training manuals for human butchery, teaching your kid strategies for becoming a savage and effective killer." Editorials in these magazines tend to glorify the blood and guts, and the ads they run feature games boasting new and unparalleled levels of savage or violent play. See for yourself.

For a refreshing alternative, take a look at *Play Right* magazine, which is devoted to the potential of video game technology.

Action Steps!

1. Be an educated consumer—learn the programs, learn the literature.

2. Develop a strict purchasing/rental policy about video games.

3. Write video game publishers and let them know what kind of games you'd like to see developed.

As the Mouse Roars

Extending Your Program to Computer Games

Computers are marvelous tools for helping us write, run our businesses, keep our finances in order, and do all sorts of things that we do in the Information Age. We use them at work, and our kids are learning how to use them in their schools. Many programs offer children unique ways to express their creativity and learn in exciting new ways. But there's a darker side to computing—a strain of games that perpetuate the violent and negative images found in the worst video games. There's also no shortage of "edutainment" software that's no real improvement over mindless children's television.

Getting Wise to Violent Computer Games

While computer games haven't gained the kind of dubious notoriety some video games have, be assured that there are plenty that allow your child to interactively save the world in a violent manner or win points through violent actions.

1. Don't buy computer games for your child just because he or she says they're cool or fun, or everyone has them—first check them out yourself. *Really play them* so you can experience all the imagery and features.

2. Peruse an issue of the electronic game magazines your child reads: You'll find overwhelming support for violent programs. "Sumo Head Butts, Sonic Booms, Whirlwind Kicks, and Butt Crushes" are just a few of the attractions that an ad for Street Fighter II promises young readers. Between articles describing strategies for more effective killing, and ads promising more opportunities to maim and kill, you need to choose your child's reading matter very carefully.

3. Explain to your child what aspects of particular games are troubling. Then take those games out of circulation. Happily, with the many thousands of commercially available programs, it's easy to find satisfying alternatives.

Selecting "Edutainment" Software

The field of educational and edutainment programs is one of the fastest-growing sectors of the software industry. Many of the new programs offer excellent opportunities for bolstering basic skills and challenging your child's mind. But others are simply games with a slight "educational" twist. Here's what you can do:

- "Test-drive" programs at retail outlets. Look for products that don't merely mimic what you can do with a book, paper, and pencil.

- Look for software *you* can get involved with, too, and even structure activities around.

- Talk to teachers and friends who use computer software. Read reviews in *Family PC Computing.* Some general computing publications occasionally review children's software as well.

- When purchasing software through the mail, buy from companies that offer a money-back guarantee.

Action Steps!

1. Pay attention to the computer action games your child plays.

2. Be critical of claims made by publishers of "edutainment" software—first try the program yourself.

3. Commend software publishers when they do a good job: They need positive feedback from the marketplace to know that they're on the right track.

Your School

Take It to School

Introducing a Schoolwide
TV-Awareness Campaign

At this point you've probably gotten television viewing under control in your own home, and you've introduced the idea of critical viewing to your family. Now how about leveraging the knowledge you've gained at home by interesting people in your school in a TV-awareness campaign?

What Is a TV-Awareness Campaign?

A television-awareness campaign consists of two components: TV turndown and training in critical viewing.

TV Turndown: The only way to change viewing habits over the long haul is to break whatever addiction is keeping parents and children glued to the set for hours on end. By demonstrating that it's possible to curb TV watching (even for only a week) by means of a "TV turndown," people can be inspired to adopt a long-term reduced-viewing program such as the one mapped out in Part II of this book. (We make no pretense that TV turndowns can permanently change viewing behaviors. Rather, they're valuable because they show people that TV doesn't have a life of its own, and that their own lives can go on with less television watching.)

Critical Viewing: Given the fact that most children will probably be allowed to watch some amount of television once the TV turndown is finished, it's important to give them tools for understanding the media they "consume." That's where media literacy comes into the picture. By making media literacy part of the TV-awareness campaign, you can introduce teachers, students, and parents to the benefits of acquiring critical-viewing skills. That exposure can translate into an effort to include media literacy training in all curricula of the school.

Together, TV turndowns and critical viewing form a powerful combination that can help your school community put television in its place, make the most vulnerable people in our society—our children—aware of the potentially harmful and exploitative messages they see on TV, and pave the way for dealing with the best and the worst of media technologies on the horizon.

The next chapter covers the general process of meeting with a principal to discuss your ideas for a television-awareness campaign, while Chapter 33 explains how to formulate goals for the campaign. Chapters 34 through 36 discuss the process of planning a TV turndown, while Chapters 37 and 38 introduce media literacy as a topic for informal class discussion and as a general element of the school curriculum.

Action Steps!

1. **Test** the waters: Ask other school parents about their interest in a TV-awareness campaign.

2. Find an interested teacher. It's always good to have an ally on the inside when you present your case to the school.

3. Roll up your sleeves and prepare for some work!

Be an Effective Torchbearer

Understanding How Schools Work

The best principals are anxious to work in partnership with parents and teachers, but to get their attention and effectively sell your idea, you need to understand their role in the school-planning process. While every principal is different and every school has a unique set of problems and politics, the basics of selling a program are the same. As Jerry Carmody, principal of the Winthrop Lower School in Melrose, Massachusetts, puts it, "The better prepared you are to explain the benefits of the program, the resources needed to achieve its purpose, and the proposed role of the principal, teachers, and parents in the program implementation, the more likely you are to gain the support needed to make your television awareness program—or any other effort—a reality in your school."

The First Meeting

The point of your first meeting with the principal is to introduce him or her to your idea and to win support. Think of it as presenting a general concept to a potential working partner, someone who will be important to your project's success. To prepare for the meeting, think about the following:

- Well-run schools plan far in advance—many plan in the spring for the upcoming school year. Make your presentation at a time when quality programming is sought.

- The purpose of the meeting is to discuss the feasibility of developing a TV-awareness program; although a detailed plan is not needed at this time (see next chapter), you should be prepared to convince your principal that, conceptually and practically, your proposed program has been well thought out.

- Tailor your presentation to your principal's style. For instance, if your principal is a "but what if . . ." type of person, you should walk in with answers to questions and resolutions to obstacles that he or she will likely pose.

- You'll need to make a convincing presentation to show that you are capable of carrying off the campaign.

- Don't be so specific that you exclude input from the teachers and administrators.

- Show support. Bring one or two other parents along. If you've enlisted the support of a teacher, try to include him or her in the meeting.

The Realities of Starting a TV-Awareness Campaign in Your School

Bear in mind the following when you approach your principal:

- The school administration's most limited resources are time and people. Be prepared to show that your program can be efficiently and effectively run without demanding a lot from school personnel.

- Your program may be viewed as an interruption. As principal Jerry Carmody points out, "No matter how good your program, you are most likely asking the principal to add it to an existing school calendar, and that can potentially impact activities or schedules already in place. You must demonstrate that the expenditure of effort and the disruption of schedules are worth it."

- Faculty support is critical, and it will come more readily if teachers are brought on board early in the planning process. While you can support and encourage teacher involvement, it's ultimately the principal's job to determine which teachers will participate in the campaign.

Action Steps!

1. Write a brief summary of your proposal for the principal.
2. Be prepared to answer specifics about the goals and implementation of the program (see next chapter).
3. Be a good salesperson, but relax.

Do Your Homework

Developing Specific Goals for the Campaign

Assuming that you've gotten support for a TV-awareness campaign, you'll need to develop a set of goals for the effort. Once you know your goals, you can back into plans for achieving them.

Questions to Ponder

Know what you want to achieve, and be prepared to state it simply and concisely. Be sure to answer these key questions:

- Who stands to benefit from the campaign? The answer will likely include more than one group—that is, students, parents, and teachers.

- What specifically do each of the groups gain? Focus on the benefits to each group. For instance, you can talk about empowering parents to feel that they have more control over television watching, about students becoming more critical viewers after the campaign, and about teachers integrating media literacy into their curricula.

- What data do you have to support the need for the program? Be sure to include hard facts about TV watching and the benefits of media literacy, as well as your personal motivation.

- What support will you require from the school for the TV turndown component of the campaign? Be clear about what you hope to get from the school during both the planning and implementation phases. If your partnership is successful, you can expect:

  - Logistics help for important elements of your campaign, such as student surveys and in-school publicity.

- School participation in a parent-support night (in the form of a room) as well as remarks by the principal or an involved faculty member.
- A student participation kickoff—think of it as a pre-game peprally.
- Teacher involvement and support in the classrooms.

- What support will the teachers require for the media literacy component of the campaign? You will need to:

  - Do the legwork. Contact some of the organizations in the resource section and have them send you sample literature, teacher's guides, etc.
  - Offer your findings, and make yourself available for further research.
  - Provide information about schools that have successfully adopted media literacy in their curricula.

Action Steps!

1. Make a short list of the benefits of your proposed program.

2. Have a casual gathering to get other parents involved.

3. Seek the support of the PTA/PTO.

4. Solicit input from teachers, counselors, and community experts.

5. Follow the steps in the next section to create a concrete game plan for the turndown.

Plan on It

Defining the Terms of Your TV Turndown

The TV turndown should support the goals you formulated in the previous chapter. The development of plans to achieve those goals should involve parents, teachers, and administrators. (The planning process is also a good way to begin generating more widespread interest and enthusiasm for the campaign.) The following questions will help you frame the planning process:

What's the Scope of Your Turndown Program?

Begin having regular get-togethers of the core group of interested parents and teachers. Your first task is to define how the turndown component will be implemented at your school.

- Some school turndown efforts involve total blackouts for a period of time. Others call for limited or selected viewing on school nights (say, news, educational, and "parent-approved" programs) or "chaperoned viewing"—parents watch with their children for a limited number of hours each week. Note that total blackouts are likely to be the least well received; many people find the idea too extreme or threatening. Know your school community before you propose your turndown goals.

- As we explained in Part II of the previous section, children will often respond best when they have some control over what they watch. You might propose that each family set a time limit, and allow children to choose from a list of shows that parents have approved.

Who's in the Cast?

The turndown doesn't necessarily have to include everyone in the school. It may be appropriate to try it first with a smaller group, such as an individual class. Often the attention the program generates will attract a broader following when it's repeated the next year. The TV Busters Program, for example, began with 19 kids in a single class in 1987. The next year, 101 out of 119 students in the school joined in. As of Spring 1993, more than 200,000 schoolchildren had participated!

When Does It Air?

Finally, decide when the turndown will start and how long it will run. Avoid holidays and school vacations. Above all, pick a realistic and achievable target that will seem reasonable to students and parents.

Action Steps!

1. Get parents and teachers involved.

2. Ask the right questions.

3. Tailor a plan to the character of your school community.

Lights, Camera, Action!

Launching Your TV Turndown

By this point you have clear objectives for your turndown and you've defined how it will work. Now it's time to take action. While every turndown will have unique elements, here are the common—and essential—actions you'll need to take to get the effort rolling.

Communicate

- Prepare and distribute information packages to parents and teachers. Include details about your campaign as well as background material on the effects of TV watching on schoolchildren and the benefits of the media literacy training that will accompany the turndown.

- Issue press releases to the local media describing the campaign and its goals—any coverage will be great inspiration for the participants.

- Arrange for a parent volunteer from each grade or class to be a contact person for information, handouts, and announcements.

- Encourage parents and teachers to discuss their concerns and successes at regular gathering times (like after-school pick-up) and special events.

Motivate

- Enlist a popular teacher to give the program an inspiring kickoff that explains how the campaign works and describes the benefits (see the next chapter for more ideas on motivating the prime participants—students).

- Develop awards and recognitions for those who participate in the campaign.

- Include fun contests such as "the most original non-TV activity" or "the most humorous essay about the event." Include parents as well.

Educate

- Involve students in the planning of the program, and discuss what you hope to accomplish.

- Provide each classroom with blank "TV Diaries," so kids can record what they watch before, during, and after the turndown.

- Pass out surveys to children, parents, and teachers about the role of TV in their lives. Share the results.

Participate

- Create lists of activities to replace TV watching. (See Section Two for suggestions.)

- Have each student keep a diary and share how he or she spends time.

- If your program runs more than one week, plan a mid-course party or event to get everyone together for a boost.

Celebrate

Have a school assembly or sponsor a celebration to conclude the program. This is a great time to hand out awards, recognize everyone's hard work, and announce the dates for the next TV-awareness campaign.

Action Steps!

1. Make an action checklist.

2. Ensure you have all items in place.

3. Launch the turndown effort!

Music to Their Ears

Selling the TV-Turndown Plan to the Students

Ultimately, the success of your turndown will depend on cooperation from the kids who take part in the effort. With a little encouragement and the right kind of support from parents and teachers, students will be surprisingly enthusiastic about the program. Above all, keep things positive. If the students view the TV-awareness campaign as a *challenge* to change their viewing behaviors and an *opportunity* to learn more about the programs they've been watching, they'll be more eager to participate. Here's some suggestions for teachers who are about to engage in "selling" a turndown program.

Yakety Yak

Remember relevance? When you were in school, everything made more sense if you could relate it to something you knew and had experienced firsthand. And hearing it from a parent or teacher was not necessarily the endorsement that moved you to action. Help students reach their own understanding about why the turndown is a good idea.

- Use the informal media literacy plan (next chapter) to open a discussion about TV in the classrooms.

- Encourage students to evaluate the impact of TV on their time and values through discussions and essays.

- If your school has a student newspaper, help the staff devote an issue to the TV-awareness campaign. Include short interviews in which students discuss the pros and cons of television.

- Accentuate the positives, such as how the campaign will give the students more time to take advantage of other activities and help them better appreciate how television and other media shape their views of the world.

Let the Good Times Roll

- Adopt a model from another event at your school that generates a lot of excitement and community support. A good example may be the big homecoming game or an intramural field day. These events have pep rallies, posters, and promotions.

- Have the principal issue a proclamation supporting the turndown. It should be addressed to the students, and it should be fun.

- Make posters, buttons, T-shirts, and special bulletin-board displays to publicize the program.

- Get the support of neighborhood merchants. For example, everybody walking into the local ice cream parlor with a TV-turndown button could be eligible for a complimentary topping.

Stand by Me

- Not every student will participate in the TV-turndown effort. Some won't have the support at home. Some may simply refuse to change their viewing habits. But even kids who continue in their old patterns can benefit from the program by learning about the effects of TV. Don't exclude them, and don't resort to negative messages. Make sure these kids don't feel ostracized.

- Give all of the students a chance to express themselves about the program—you may be able to help kids overcome obstacles once you've heard them.

Action Steps!

1. Encourage student discussion about TV watching.

2. Plan events to raise awareness of and promote the program.

3. Keep everyone informed—even the skeptics.

Talk About the Tube

Helping Students to Understand
TV Messages

With everyone's attention focused on curbing television watching, teachers can take the opportunity to discuss media issues in the classroom. While the ultimate goal should be an approach that incorporates critical-viewing skills throughout the curriculum, it's easy to start with an informal discussion. The only prerequisite is that teachers become comfortable with the media itself. "You can't pretend television doesn't exist or exert a powerful influence on students," cautions Dr. Parker Page, president of the Children's Television Resource and Education Center (C-TREC, see resources section). "And you can't worry that talking about television will encourage more watching—it's IMPOSSIBLE for students to watch any more than they do!" To help teachers conduct informal discussions, C-TREC recommends the following (adapted with permission from *TV Breakout #2: Children and TV: What Teachers Can Do*):

1. During small-group or class discussion time, find out which programs your students watch most often. Talk about:

   - What the students like and dislike about the characters.
   - Which TV characters use put-downs, and why.
   - Whether the students ever wish they were a certain TV character.
   - How they can tell when things on TV are real or unreal.
   - Whether the students worry about situations they see on TV.
   - How truthful students believe commercials to be.

2. Use the answers as a point of departure for further discussion. For example, you might discuss:

- What is a hero?
- Why are some cartoon- or action/adventure-show characters called "superheroes"?
- Can heroes be helpful without being violent?

3. Have students carry out follow-up activities such as:

- Bringing in pictures or stories from magazines, newspapers, or the evening TV news about people doing something heroic or helpful without being violent.
- Asking their families to write down a heroic act performed by someone they know. The students can illustrate the stories and share them with the rest of the class. Pictures of each story can be featured on a Real Superheroes bulletin board.
- Selecting one child (or more) who has been helpful or "heroic" recently as Hero(es) of the Week.

4. Conduct a summary discussion to:

- Review what students have said and done.
- Recall specific examples of stories and artwork.
- Ask what the students think a superhero is now. Is it different from what they thought before? Why or why not?

Now use your imagination to apply the same line of inquiry to other topics important to your students' world and the lessons you're trying to teach.

Action Steps!

1. Find out which shows are popular in your class.

2. Watch the shows with a nonjudgmental eye.

3. Spark a discussion and follow-up talks.

The Complete Curriculum

Jump-Starting a Schoolwide Media Literacy Campaign

Informal discussions about media issues and messages can whet everyone's appetite for a more formal approach to teaching critical-viewing skills. How can you sell your school on the idea, so that critical viewing becomes an integral part of the curriculum? Dr. David Considine, professor of media in the College of Education at Appalachian State University and co-author of *Visual Messages: Integrating Imagery into Instruction* (see resource section), suggests that parents can act as important agents of change through their PTA/PTO organizations. When presenting information to the school about integrating a media literacy curriculum:

- Identify resources that can help. There's no point in reinventing the wheel; numerous organizations can provide you with information about schoolwide media-literacy curricula and what other schools and districts have done.

- Find allies, and begin building a critical mass. Don't preach to the converted or the ostriches, Considine advises. He also recommends focusing on health educators. They are traditionally concerned with alcohol, tobacco consumption, substance abuse, nutrition/diet, and adolescent sexuality—all issues addressed by media literacy.

- Develop a strong case that you can present to the decision makers within your school or school system. Your case should stress that:

  - Media literacy is a response to the social reality of the communications revolution, in which jobs will be acquired on the basis of one's ability to analyze, access, evaluate, and produce meaningful information.

  - Somewhere in the school's mission statement will be wording to the effect that "our aim is to produce responsible citizens for a democratic society." And in a media society, responsible citizens must understand the way media of all types shape their perceptions, their awareness of other countries and cultures, their understanding of the world at large, and their sense of who they are. In other words, media literacy is compatible with the fundamental goals of the school.

Suggestions for Getting Your Ideas Accepted

- Make it your goal to initiate a dialogue with school officials. If you package your ideas in the form of a demand, you can be guaranteed a negative response.

- Talk with parents and educators in schools that have implemented top-to-bottom media-literacy campaigns (contact the National Telemedia Council or the other organizations listed in the resource section).

- Anticipate the concerns and questions of all your stakeholders, and develop meaningful responses. Some parents might wonder why the school is using its resources to address media literacy rather than adding a more "worthwhile" academic subject to the curriculum. Familiarize yourself with the main benefits of media literacy—helping students become "TV-smart," so they'll be less influenced by the negative effects of television, and they'll become better consumers of ALL media.

Action Steps!

1. Become literate about media literacy—see the resource section.

2. Identify like-minded people in your PTA/PTO.

3. Begin building your critical mass of support.

4. Share your knowledge through civic, religious, and other organizations so that other communities can begin to adopt media literacy curricula in their school systems.

Your Community

Speak Up!

Getting Involved in the Change Process

Throughout this book we've provided tools for helping you change
the amount of time your family
members spend watching TV and
for helping them become critical
viewers. We've also described
how to apply the change process
to your school. Now, if you're so
inclined, think about fostering
changes in the media itself.

Changing TV for Our Kids

There are lots of ways to bring about change; the key is to do it in a
way in which all sides perceive themselves to be winners. Here are
some thoughts on how to achieve productive change in television
and other media.

1. Avoid censorship. "It's terribly important for parents and teachers to remember that the solution to terrible speech is MORE
   speech," says Peggy Charren, the midwife of the Children's Television Act (see Chapter 41) and an internationally recognized
   advocate for improving children's television. "No one thinks it's
   healthy for kids to see the kind of horrible images they see today.
   But when you end up censoring the media, you end up living in
   the kind of country you have to move out of."

2. Use available tools to ensure compliance with the law. Says
   Charren, "Broadcasting is a local institution that uses a public

commodity—the airwaves. In return for the privilege of using the airwaves, we require broadcasters to serve the public interest. Compliance with the Children's Television Act will not only result in the kind of educational and informational programming that we seek for our children, but it will give us choice. And choice is what living in a democracy is all about."

3. Think smart business. People who produce commercial television shows, video games, and other media primarily want to make money. So if you want to see new offerings, become part of a campaign to initiate a dialogue with TV producers, video game makers and software publishers, and others in the media industry. Show them that great marketplace opportunities exist for alternatives to the kinds of shows and products constantly under fire from the press and the government. Our wallets provide strong incentives for change.

Changing Media for Everyone

In the following two chapters, you'll learn about a national strategy for bringing about improved compliance with the Children's Television Act, as well as an example of its implementation on a statewide basis. In reading these chapters, think about how you can extend the principles and tactics beyond children's television to the improvement of media products for people of all ages.

Action Steps!

1. Ask friends about their interest in working for change at the grassroots level.

2. Identify community organizations—religious groups, PTA/PTOs, rotary clubs, etc.—that share your concern.

3. Encourage people to make a commitment to getting involved.

Grassroots Community Action

Talking Back to Your Television Set

"Parents feel pretty powerless about television—it seems to control their lives at so many levels. But the fact is, there are many things that we, as citizens, can do to bring about change in our local communities." So says Dr. Kathryn Montgomery, president of the Washington, DC-based Center for Media Education (CME) (see resources section, "Watchdog Groups"). Dr. Montgomery recommends the following actions:

- Sponsor "Media Literacy Nights" that educate people about the effects of television and television law. Every community has an expert on TV and other media, whether he or she is a professor of communications at a local university, a mental health professional, a pediatrician, or a PTA member steeped in the literature about television. Use a school, church, or town meeting hall. CME can provide technical support materials for launching the meeting.

- Create a forum in which broadcasters and experts can sit at the same table. Sometimes local TV station managers are unaware of how the content of the programs they air can affect viewers. Station managers, experts, and parents can screen tapes of shows recently aired and then discuss concerns.

- Prepare literature—simple bulletins, brochures, newsletters—that educates people about the law (for instance, how many minutes of advertising can be shown during children's television programs, or how commercials must be differentiated from the actual program). CME can provide basic information about FCC regulations.

- Initiate a letter-writing campaign to local broadcasters: TV stations are highly sensitive to public pressure. Avoid form letters, which tend to be dismissed. Rather, circulate a list of key points that letters should address. Letters from local experts will also bolster the campaign.

- Get your local press involved. You don't have to land on the cover of *Time* or *Newsweek* to make a difference. Get local reporters to cover the community's feelings about issues such as TV violence and the airing of more programs with valid educational content. Sometimes your local print media can provide a wake-up call to TV stations.

- Set up monitoring teams. Seek volunteers to periodically monitor the local airwaves for infractions of the law. Include retirees and other people with flexible schedules. These teams can eventually issue "Report Cards" that rate local stations in terms of children's programming and other key issues (see the next chapter for details).

Action Steps!

1. Meet with your neighbors and form a core committee.

2. Agree on a limited number of "doable" projects, such as an education night or letter-writing campaign.

3. Break down the projects into specific tasks, create a plan for accomplishing them, and begin the grassroots advocacy process.

Pass/Fail

Grading Your Local Television Station

Question: Which of the following television shows would you classify as serving the educational and informational needs of your children: *Leave It to Beaver*, GI Joe cartoons, or the adventures of Bucky O'Hare (the laser-gun-toting cartoon rabbit who fights alien toads)?

Most of us would probably answer, "None of the above." Believe it or not, though, a number of broadcasters are claiming "*All* of the above!"

Since the passage of the Children's Television Act, broadcasters (not cable stations) have been required to provide programming that furthers the positive development of the child in some respect, including his or her "cognitive/intellectual or emotional/social needs." Even within this loose set of guidelines, the idea of Bucky O'Hare as educational or informational is absurd. The act also limits commercial time in children's programming (i.e., programming aimed at children 12 years of age and younger) to 10.5 minutes per hour on weekends and 12 minutes on weekdays—a limit that's sometimes exceeded.

What can you and your neighbors do about flagrant violations of the act? "Plenty," says Charlene Hughins Uhl, director of Ready at Five, a youth advocacy organization participating in Maryland's Campaign for Kids' TV. "You have a lot of leverage as viewers in a community."

Ready at Five, with one of its partners, Advocates for Children and Youth, was the first state-wide organization to apply the children's programming evaluation process developed by the Center for Media Education (see resource section). CME believes that the impact of television is greatest at the local community level, so a consistent evaluation strategy used by communities across the country will have the greatest chance of bringing about compliance with the act.

You can apply CME's strategy to your community by taking the following steps:

1. Identify groups that share an interest in television issues: your PTA/PTO, church, Boy Scout or Girl Scout group, etc. As Uhl puts it, "With TV sets in more than 92 percent of American households, television issues cut across all cultural and socio-economic boundaries, so you're bound to find an interested partner."

2. Divvy up the TV stations—each group should pick one or two to monitor.

3. Visit local stations and review the public inspection file, which is supposed to contain a log of what the stations air in response to the Children's Television Act.

4. Tape the educational/informational shows and view them as a team.

5. Score the programs on educational content, the positive portrayal of racial and ethnic groups, conflict resolution, and other important issues (see page 120 for a copy of the Maryland programming worksheet). Average the scores for the shows.

6. Visit the stations again and tell the managers your findings. "Don't go in with the attitude that you're making a judgment," Uhl cautions. "That will just lead to defensiveness. Make it clear that you're trying to initiate a dialogue, not censure anyone, and you'll get more cooperation."

7. Take your findings to the rest of the community. Uhl's organization chose to issue a "Report Card" for local stations. "The Report Card generated a phenomenal amount of local and national press," she says. "But don't underestimate the power of a good letter-writing campaign—it can be a great way to achieve your goals!"

Action Steps!

1. Meet with friends and neighbors and discuss how they could get involved in monitoring local programming.

2. Compile a list of local organizations, then enlist their support.

3. Contact CME and launch your campaign.

Postscript

Perils and Opportunities on
the Media Road Ahead

Technologies that boggle the mind are rapidly being developed, and new challenges await all of us concerned about media. More than ever, we'll have to work hard to ensure that media serve our needs, rather than simply amplify the worst of today's television and video games. The stakes will be too high to leave matters in the hands of faceless conglomerates that have a purely commercial interest.

Take the so-called "information superhighway" already in use. When everyone can tune in to 500 cable stations, what will be available on their screens? Will the offerings truly be tailored to the educational and informational needs of children and adults? Will the programs support the cultural diversity of the communities they serve? Or will the highway be littered with storefronts making up the greatest electronic shopping mall on the planet, a mall designed to exploit the most lucrative and vulnerable of all markets: our children? Big screens. Big choices. Big impact.

And what of virtual reality, which blurs the line between the human mind and the machine? Virtual reality creates a level of entertainment opportunities unparalleled by any current video or interactive games. Though in development now, it's coming to your toy store and living room all too soon.

Players of virtual-reality games wear a helmet that displays a scene in which they can actively participate; they are not just manipulating images. As they move the controls, all their senses tell their brains that they're actually interacting with the animate and inanimate objects they encounter. As therapist Carleton Kendrick puts it, "Virtual reality is the ultimate in 'multi-sensate, hypnotic frames of mind.' It affords people the chance to purchase as close to an out-of-body experience as they can without obtaining illegal drugs."

If violence continues to be the predominant theme in interactive games, the implications for virtual-reality games are frightening. Cautions Kendricks, "When your child removes the helmet after decapitating or disemboweling an opponent, he'll have the sweat of death on his brow. Save for actual blood dripping from his sword, in his mind he WILL have committed a savage act of murder."

Act now before the technology hits the shelves. Use the political process to ensure that all of us have rich viewing choices. Create marketplace demand for media products that make the best of new technologies, rather than exploiting violence, sex, and other themes that are inexpensive to produce and easy to export. In short, we must shape the media future while we can, instead of waiting for it to be handed to us on a plate.

SECTION TWO

TV-Free Activities

Books, **42** Books, Books

Your family probably has stacks of magazines and books at home. The library provides unlimited access to even more. Here's how you can make the most of them for learning, exploring, and enjoying.

Books at Home

Write a Sequel. Do you ever wonder what happens after the storybook ends? Well, have your family continue the plots of their favorite books, adding a variety of situations and characters. Who knows, the sequel might be better than the original!

Draw a Book Report. Here's a project the whole family can enjoy: Draw five pictures that synopsize the plots of some family favorites. Then have each family member present his or her "report" and see if everyone else can name the book.

Meet the Characters. Your child may have given oral book reports before, but has he or she ever done so from the perspective of the author? Ask your child to pretend that he or she has penned a favorite book and then express insights about the characters that only the author can offer.

Five Stars. Does your family have strong opinions about books? Schedule book review sessions, and use them to steer family members toward books that are not already household runaway successes.

Act the Part. Choose a favorite storybook with some great characters, and cast family members in the major roles. Then have your family read the book aloud—with each person portraying a leading character.

Shake Hands. How would you like to see your favorite storybook characters resolve their differences of opinion? Assign family members antagonist/protagonist roles (Peter Pan and Captain Hook, for instance). Then let the characters talk things out, make up, and shake hands.

Library Adventures

Believe It or Not. Have your family members explore the periodical section of your local library and compile lists of strange facts and stories. Then at home your family can share the "real scoop!"

Birthday History. Have your family scan back copies of newspapers and magazines to find out what events were happening in the world on the days they were born.

Meet the Authors. Send your family members on a fact-finding mission in the reference section of the library. Have them compile biographies of their favorite writers. Later, have each participant portray the author he or she researched at a "meet the authors" party.

Story Inspirations. Have your family members "collect" (jot down) interesting book titles, newspaper headlines, and magazine article titles. Then sponsor a family storytelling hour—with participants spinning tales around their collection of story "ideas."

About the Town. How much does your family know about the city or town where you live? Prepare a list of questions in advance (when and why the town was founded, who built the first home, and so on), and see how many of the answers your sleuths can uncover at the library.

Book Grab Bag. At home, have each participant draw the name of another family member out of a hat. Now send the family on a "library shopping trip" to choose three books for designated recipients. How well do members of your family know one another's reading tastes?

Museum Explorations

You and your family can always learn something at a nearby museum—whether this is your first visit there or your fiftieth. Try adding these new twists to a favorite pastime:

Alphabetical Hunt. You've seen museum exhibits—but have you ever seen them in alphabetical order? Have your family work as a team to find objects (or, if you're at an art museum, perhaps artists' names) from A to Z.

Can You Find It? Make a list of items to be found in the museum, and send your family on a scavenger hunt. Now, did anyone find the painting of the dog in the red sneakers?

Nomadic Numbers. Encourage your family to wander through the entire museum finding examples of numbers—in order, of course! You might see two headdresses in a case, three umbrellas in a painting, and so on. Best of all, your family can count on having a good time.

Mystery Object. Before your museum trip, think of a "mystery object" and give your family hints as to its identity. For example, you might reveal that "the object's first letter is an *r* and the last a *t*, and it's on the third floor in the west wing." Then your family's museum adventure can take off, well, like a rocket!

Take-a-Break Game. Does your family need to sit down and rest for a bit? Then try this. Say, "I spy something blue," and see who can spot the blue object. The person with the correct guess then says "I spy" another type of object. The game can continue until it's time for your museum adventure to resume.

Describe It. In this game, one person gives clues about an object in the room or exhibit, and the rest of the players ask questions to get more information until they determine the object. So who *is* that dark-haired woman with the mysterious smile?

Seeing Double. Have your family members find similarities between two objects vastly different from each other—the more different, the more fun!

Quick Study. Does your family have a great collective memory? Have the group look at objects, exhibit cases, or paintings for a pre-determined amount of time (say, two minutes) and then ask them to turn their backs. Can they pass a quiz on the details?

Bluff Masters. Can your family separate museum facts from innovative fictions? Have one person turn his or her back to an object while everyone else takes turns "explaining" the object (how it works, who invented it, etc.), with all but one player offering silly explanations. Can your "guesser" identify the designated family truth-teller?

Can You Compare Them? Have your museum goers compare one item in an exhibit with another that either looks similar or can be used for the same purpose. Or perhaps compare an ancient artifact with something we see or use in modern life. So how do those Etruscan cooking utensils stack up against the kitchen gear you used to cook dinner last night?

Homemade Toys and Games

Your house is chock-full of new toys and games. All your family has to do is invent them! (Please note, however, that some of the following activities involve small items that are not appropriate for young children. Supervise carefully.)

Gameboard. Make your own gameboard complete with colored spaces, obstacles, pitfalls, and playing cards. Have your child invent his or her own rules. Back-chesi, anyone?

Towel Tube Rocket. Have your kids glue "fins" and a nose cone on an empty paper towel tube, decorate it, and head for outer space!

Counter's List. Find things at home that "add up to" a numbered list. For example, you may have one refrigerator, two bathtubs, three chairs, and four smoke detectors. You may even have five family members!

Invent a Machine. Start with an empty box, and glue on plastic lids, bottle caps, buttons, metal washers, pipe cleaners, pictures, bits of string, cardboard arrows, and anything else your kids can imagine. This machine can do anything!

Town Layout. Roll out a large sheet of kraft paper or newsprint, and create a town. Add small boxes for buildings and cars, and draw streets, sidewalks, playgrounds, and so on. Now you're ready to move in!

Coffee Can Drum. An empty coffee can with a plastic lid is a drum, and a honey dipper or wooden spoon is a drumstick. You now have the beginnings of a parade.

Bingo. Make simple bingo cards with letters across the top and numbers down the side. Take turns pulling slips from a large bowl and mark your spaces with buttons. Bingo!

Homemade Memory Game. Glue similar pictures from magazines onto small paper or cardboard squares in matching pairs. Mix them up, lay them out facedown, and concentrate! Can you turn over a matching picture pair?

Find Those Things. Do your kids know where household objects, important and obscure, reside today? Name an item, and have your kids guess where it is (they can then go and check). Now, do you know the whereabouts of your children's toys? Does anyone?

Pasta Pick-Up Sticks. Play pick-up sticks with uncooked spaghetti. Hold the sauce!

Sorting Race. Fill a bowl with a lot of small items: dry beans, pasta, nuts, etc. Run time trials to see who can sort them out in an empty ice-cube tray more quickly than last time. As a variation, do the sorting blindfolded!

Costume Hunt. Hide dress-up items around the house, and have your kids find and put them on. Make the search more interesting by marking items with stick-on labels, so each child has his or her own set to locate.

Do-It-Yourself Cards. Turn some thin cardboard or index cards into a personalized set of playing cards. Hey, that king looks a lot like Dad, doesn't he?

Shake-It Toy. Can you guess an object by the way it sounds? Have your children put a small object into a box or brown bag, close it, and shake it around. Now, can you identify that rattle?

Easy Sports

Your family is a great team, even without team shirts and lots of expensive equipment. Here are some sports you can enjoy anytime.

Plastic Lid Frisbee Golf. Set a series of plastic bowls or saucepans around the house, with a numbered tag on each one. The object of the game is to throw (Frisbee style) a small plastic lid into the targets in the numbered order. How many tosses will it take to complete a round?

Bag-Target Ball Toss. Use concentric circles cut from paper bags to make a target on the floor. Mark each circle with a color or number, and toss foam balls (or wadded-up pieces of paper) onto the target to score points. Can anyone get a bull's-eye?

Pitching "Quarters." This is an adaptation of an old city sidewalk game. Each player throws a "quarter" (actually, a plastic lid or button) toward a wall. The one that lands nearest the wall wins, and the thrower keeps all the "coins"—until the next toss.

Beanbag Juggle. Would your kids like to join a homemade circus? Place half a cup of dried navy beans in a sandwich bag, tie the bag, then put the bag in an old sock. Tie the sock closed. Now you have a beanbag for juggling or just clowning around.

Pinball Wizards. Use boxes, books, and blocks to create an obstacle course (a hallway is the best location). Take turns rolling a light ball through the course to see who can get it to the other end in a single roll. Proclaim that person a "pinball wizard."

Giant Billiards. Pool, anyone? Use wrapping paper tubes for cue sticks. Tape paper bags or shoe boxes to table corners for "pockets." Supply several foam balls, and rack 'em up!

Spoonful of Beans. Can the runners, hoppers, and crawlers in your home complete relay races while holding a spoonful of beans? If any spill, don't put them in tonight's soup!

Crazy Mazes. Budding balance-beam gymnasts and tightrope walkers can hone their skills by walking along a piece of string or rope. For a real challenge, loop the "line" into an intricate maze.

Cup Catch. Tired of regular catch? Try playing it with Ping-Pong balls, using paper cups (the ones with fold-out handles are great). Those sure are strange-looking catcher's mitts!

Onion Bag Dodgeball. Fill an empty onion bag (the strong mesh type) with crumpled-up newspaper, and tie it closed. Split your group into two teams, and stand on opposite sides of a line. The idea is to toss the "ball" at your opponents. A hit removes the player from the game. If you catch the ball, you're safe—until the next round.

Theme Putt-Putt. Create your own indoor miniature golf course with a theme. Use empty containers for "holes," furniture for obstacles, and toys for scenery and props (dinosaurs, trees, etc.). Long cardboard tubes can be turned into putters. Fore!

Indoor Hopscotch. Remember chalking hopscotch grids on the sidewalk? Have your kids make an indoor version using kraft paper (taped to the floor) and crayons. And the rain will never wash it away.

Arts and Crafts

Get out the scissors and glue! Save that scrap paper! Da Vinci had nothing on your kids when it comes to enthusiasm for art. Ready, set, create!

Homespun-Art Museum. If your home has an empty wall, why not turn it into an art museum? Encourage art projects by keeping materials—crayons, washable markers, scrap paper, etc.—on hand. As your child creates a number of "masterpieces," display them on the wall. Now your child can take visitors on a guided tour of the homespun-art museum.

Story Collage. Have your child pick a familiar setting, like your town, a favorite vacation spot, or Grandma's house, where the story can take place. He or she can cut pictures out of magazines to illustrate the setting. Next, make up a plot, and glue down the pictures to tell the story.

Diorama Drama. This project can be informative, silly, or both. Cut out and glue scenery in a large shoebox set on its side. Now add people and animals, and small toys. Say, why is that truck driving down the left side of that cloud?

Trace Your Stuff. For this activity, you'll need an assortment of traceable household objects: jar lids, cookie cutters, and maybe some shapes of your own cut from cardboard. Have your kids trace the items to make pictures, add details, and who knows—your children might even invent the world's first banana-peel recycler!

Note Holder. Have your kids make a gift for someone special by decorating a piece of cardboard and gluing on a clothespin near the top. Then help them cut small pieces of paper to clip on for notes. Add a string or yarn, and attach a pen. Write on!

Family Portraits. Having a theme can make drawing portraits especially interesting for your kids. Challenge them to draw pictures of each member of the family doing a favorite activity or dressed as their favorite character. Now hang the portraits in a place of honor.

Art of the Month. Do you have an extra calendar? Have your kids personalize it. They can replace the photos with art of their own based on seasonal or holiday themes: Valentine's Day for February, the beach for August, and so on. Do you suppose they'll have any ideas for their birthday month?

Personalized Placemats. This idea may get the kids interested in setting the table. Have your child decorate a large sheet of heavy paper, add the artist's photo, and cover it with clear contact paper. Each artist can eat off of his or her own work.

Wearable Art. Are your kids tired of their clothes? Then give them some fabric paint and markers. Your kids can decorate old sneakers, hats, or T-shirts or other items you deem appropriate. Be sure your kids understand their designs are permanent—these paints are not made to wash out.

Make a Frame. Buy simple cardboard frames for photos, or cut out your own from pasteboard or scrap cardboard. Let the kids decorate them with paint, markers, glitter, etc. Use the finished products for favorite family photographs or homemade masterpieces.

Parties and Celebrations

Is your family looking for an excuse to celebrate? Here are some reasons—and ideas—for throwing memorable parties. Now let the good times roll!

Anytime Trick-or-Treat. Your family can celebrate Halloween anytime during the year. Simply don some interesting costumes, accessories, makeup, and masks. You can almost see the pumpkins!

The "A" List. Which celebrities would your family members most want to rub shoulders with? Throw a bash for the "A"-list partygoers, with your family portraying the famous folks.

Chocolate Chip Cookie–Tasting Party. Get a sample of several leading brands of chocolate chip cookies, as well as your own home-made favorites. Now conduct "taste research" with the taster's eyes closed. See how refined those palates really are.

Medieval Merriment. Invite kings, queens, knights, court jesters, and other characters from the Middle Ages into a party at your castle. And don't forget the ginger ale!

Meet the Characters. Choose a story, cast family members in particular roles, and invite the characters to a party at your place. What a novel idea!

Fun Fundraiser. Pick some silly causes and throw a party that revolves around two or more incongruous issues, like Elect Our Cat and Save Our Doorknobs. (Or, to follow in the footsteps of the infamous Click and Clack on the national "Car Talk" show, Save the Skeets!)

Pantomime Party. Throw a get-together with a twist: All of the guests must be mimes. See if you can pantomime your way through refreshments, gift giving, and games. Remember—shhhh!

Guest of Honor. Have a series of parties, each honoring a different family member. Recognize recent accomplishments with certificates and speeches. Isn't it great to be appreciated?

Not-Here Party. Have a party somewhere besides where you live. Turn your home into another city, country, or even planet. For your lunar gig, bring in the snow saucers for craters, assemble a wrapping paper tube dwelling, and serve green "cheese."

The "What?" Party. Go to the library and locate an upcoming holiday that no one in your family has likely heard of. Make invitations for family members and start a whole new tradition!

"Ago" Go-Go. Have your family members choose a prehistoric time period, and hold a party in that era. Maybe you can enjoy a Jurassic Celebration, an Ice-Age Get-Together, or a Bronze-Age Bash!

Dessert-Tasting Party. Grownups have wine tastings—why can't your family have a "dessert tasting"? Simply assemble your favorite desserts (make-believe or real), and have your tasters sample the treats. What's the favorite in your houshold?

Performing Arts

Why not turn your home into a theater and encourage the acting, singing, and other talents of your family "hams"? After all, everyone deserves his or her time in the spotlight!

Mime a Sport. Turn in a fun performance—and circumvent the "don't play ball in the house" rule at the same time. Have your family pantomime a soccer game, a tennis tournament, or another sports event. Everyone wins!

Vaudeville Extravaganza. Organize a catchall arts revue, and let the singers, dancers, acrobats, mimes, musicians, and actors in your family "strut their stuff." And after you've had your turn "on stage," sit back and enjoy the show.

Family Theme Song. Compose a song that captures the spirit of your family. Have everyone take turns contributing lyrics that describe family members, trips, activities, and so on. Then it's time to perform it—you might even want to record the final version.

Instant Ballet. Even if your family isn't yet ready to perform at Lincoln Center, you can still translate a favorite story into dance. Cast a familiar tale, and have each family member "choreograph" his or her own role. Then clear some space and begin the ballet.

Clown Around. Gather some old hats, shoes, clothes, gloves, and makeup, and turn members of your family into circus performers. The greater your assortment of costumes, the more variety in your cast of clowns.

Sneak Preview. Is there an exciting or worrisome upcoming event, such as a family trip, the first day of school, or a visit to the dentist? Have your family turn the event into a skit, with each "actor" improvising his or her own version of the future.

A Chorus Line. How would your family like to practice the art form that made the Rockettes famous? Have your family stand in a line, and synchronize simple movements (turns, leg kicks, arm raising, etc.). Radio City Hall, here we come!

Pseudo Shakespeare. Is your family ready for the ultimate acting challenge? Grab a phone book or junk mail catalogue, and have family members take turns offering "dramatic readings." You might just start a whole new wave of experimental theater.

Time Warp. What will your kids be like in twenty years? Have each "actor" age him- or herself a couple of decades (makeup, costumes, and props are optional), and then improvise a skit starring your cast of "older" characters.

Mystery Monologue. Have your child pretend to be a storybook character and tell you a little about him- or herself. Other family members can ask questions about the character's life and guess his or her identity.

Fashion Show. Do you have any cutting-edge fashion designers in your family? Have each participant pull together one or more interesting outfits. Then have family members take turns modeling and describing their creations.

Anytime Improv. Stage an instant play, inventing the script and miming the props as you go along. Let each family member be an important part of the ensemble.

Family Press

How would your family members like to discover the power of the press while expanding their journalistic and artistic talents? All it takes is some paper, pens or pencils, crayons or markers, paints, a stapler—and a little time and imagination.

Certificates of Merit. Everybody deserves a pat on the back every now and then. Have each participant choose a family member (perhaps by selecting names out of a hat) and design a special award to honor him or her for a recent achievement (say, for putting toys away). Then, emcee a family awards night and present the certificates.

Read All About Us! How would you like to create a "public relations" brochure about your family? Fold a sheet of paper into thirds, and have each participant design a panel about a family member (prewriters can illustrate the text). And don't forget to title the brochure with a snappy headline that captures your family's true spirit.

Create the Comics. If your family members have some artistic talents, why not put them to work designing a comic book? You might have each participant work on a page individually, or you can ask younger children to draw the pictures while older kids and grownups write the text. Then staple the book together so your children can share their great works with friends.

In the News. Has your family been following current events in the community, the country, or the world? Have each participant write a paragraph or two about a recent happening and draw a picture to use as an illustration. Then fold the pages together newspaper style, and try reading aloud all the news that's fit to print.

Family Magazine. Would your family like to be featured in a magazine? Simply have an "editor" assign stories to "reporters"—say, about school, work, or a recent or upcoming family vacation. Then have your reporters submit their work, staple it together, and find out why your family is so famous.

Freehand Photo Album. Here's an assignment for the artists in your family: Have them draw pictures of themselves or other family members. Or give each person a task, such as drawing somebody at school or sketching the family at Thanksgiving dinner. Then staple all of the "snapshots" together. And don't forget to add captions for each "photo."

Birthday Book. Here's a great gift that family members can make for one another's birthdays. Have each participant write and illustrate a page of a story, making sure to use the name of the birthday boy or girl at least once on every page. Then design a cover, and staple the manuscript. Now you have a truly personalized birthday gift.

Numbers Book. Here's a way to help younger children learn their numbers while making another book to add to their collection. Give your child ten sheets of paper, and ask him or her to write a number (from one to ten) on every page. Next, have your child draw as many items as needed to match each number: one duck, two houses, three flowers, and so on. "Bind" the book with a staple and add it to your family library.

Holiday Newsletter. Would distant relatives and friends enjoy hearing your family's news during the holiday season? Have your family members put together a newsletter (that you can later photocopy and mail) about seasonal activities, trips, games, and other projects. Make sure to add illustrations. Newsletters should be seen as well as heard.

Postcards from the Press. Postcards are the simplest items for your family press to produce—and the least expensive to mail. So why not make a pile? Have each family member illustrate, address, write a message, and place a stamp on an appropriately sized piece of heavy paper (with your supervision, if necessary). Then take a family trip to the post office, and wait for some responses from your friends and relatives.

The Audio/Video Squad

Want to take revenge on the media industry? Then have your kids use a tape recorder or video camera (perhaps rent one for the occasion) to produce, direct, and star in their own productions. (With smaller kids, set the video camera up on a tripod for safety.)

Tape Recorders

Attention, Sports Fans. Record your own play-by-play commentary for your favorite sports event. You can create an imaginary game or describe a real one. John Madden, move over!

Talk Radio. Invite your family and friends to be interviewed on your radio talk show. Or have them "phone in" comments. Light up that switchboard!

Books-on-Tape. Older kids will get a kick out of recording a book reading for younger siblings. Add a bell or click to let pre-readers know when to turn the page of an illustrated storybook, and they can follow along.

Travel Instructions. Have the kids walk around the house with a portable tape recorder and describe their route. Then pass the tape along to someone else and see whether he or she can duplicate the walk without getting lost.

What Do You Hear? Take turns recording sounds around the house, such as water running and light switches clicking. Then play the tape and see who can guess what made the noises. What *was* that strange gurgling sound?

Recorded Greetings. Tape a "letter" (have the kids prepare what they want to say ahead of time) for someone who lives far away. Songs, jokes, etc., can liven up the recording. Roll tape!

Mood Music. Wouldn't read-aloud time be even more exciting if you had some melodies to enhance the narration? Have your children record some "mood music," and play it next time you read a story.

Video Recorders

Grow a Building. How does your building grow? Simply set the camera on a tripod aimed at a Lego or wooden block construction site. Place a piece on your structure, film for two seconds, pause the recorder, add another piece, and so on.

Silly Polls. Have the kids question friends and neighbors about a nonsense topic, such as: "When it's raining, do you prefer vanilla or chocolate ice cream?" Videotape their responses and, of course, their quizzical looks.

Video Diary. Want to know what your kids have been up to? Pick a regular weekly or biweekly time to set up your video camera and have the kids talk about any exciting happenings at school or in the neighborhood.

TV Spoof. Have your kids film a spoof of a TV show. Then have everyone sit down for a viewing—we're all used to seeing silliness on the tube!

Instructional Video. Have your kids create their own "how-to" video for cooking a special dish, doing an arts-and-crafts project, etc. Maybe you'll even learn how to use that computer.

Educational TV. Older kids can create a video related to something they're studying at school, such as recycling, politics, other cultures, etc. What current events are "hot" in your family?

Local Travelogue. Kids can make tapes describing places they know well, starting with their own home. Older kids can make a video "tour" of the neighborhood. You won't need to visit your local video store to take your next travelogue trip.

Zany Television

There's only one way we know of to find "quality" television programming: "Broadcast" your own! You can turn a large cardboard box into a TV by cutting out a rectangular hole for a "screen," cutting a door in the back, and having your kids draw dials and buttons with crayons, paints, etc. Now, on with the show!

Debate of the Decade. If you can fit two "candidates" inside your homemade television, then why not hold a political debate? For an even greater challenge, have your politicians try to stick to the issues!

Another Planet. What if your homemade television could pick up signals from outer space? Have your family members take turns "broadcasting" news programs, commercials, dramas, etc., from another planet. Now, back to Neptune!

Good News Channel. Maybe good news doesn't grab the headlines, but it can occupy an entire channel on your homemade television! Have your family collect (or invent) stories of kind deeds, happy endings, or lucky breaks—and then put the good news on the air.

Puppet Players. Do you have any budding puppeteers in your family? Have them present an all-puppet show (perhaps the ventriloquists can stay out of sight while the puppets enjoy the spotlight). Get ready for the puppet news at six!

Cookie Kitchen. Have your child/chef show "viewers" how to mix ingredients, roll dough, and cut out, bake, and decorate cookies in all shapes and sizes. (This should be "make-believe," of course—you wouldn't want to decorate your TV studio with cookie dough!)

Fireside Chat. How would you like to see a former United States president—say, Abraham Lincoln—deliver a television speech about an issue in our modern world? Have your family members portray the presidents and turn the impossible into the entertaining.

Silly Shopping Network. Have your family members pitch pet rubberbands and other useless products on your zany television network. No doubt your pretend phone lines will start ringing off the hook.

FTV. Broadcast an all-music TV station with a twist: no offensive lyrics or violence. Now that's family television!

Wishful Weather Channel. Does your family dream of snow in July or a rainstorm in the desert? Then have your "meteorologists" broadcast their fantasy weather patterns. Who knows—you might find yourselves taking your swimsuits and going to a New England beach in December.

Sports Shorts. If your family members are sports fans, have them take turns reporting fantasy scores. Maybe your local baseball team really will win the World Series—on your homemade television, at least.

Family Fix-It. Here's a chance for your family members to show off their skills at repairing and restoring household items. Best of all, your handy-people can improvise the sounds of drills, saws, and other tools.

TV-VIEWING LOG

Day of the week: _____

Date: _____

Name:	N:		N:		N:		N:		N:	
Time On	:		:		:		:		:	
Time Off	:		:		:		:		:	
Time Watched	hrs	min	hrs	min	hrs	min	hrs	min	hrs	min
Name of Show										
Time On	:		:		:		:		:	
Time Off	:		:		:		:		:	
Time Watched	hrs	min	hrs	min	hrs	min	hrs	min	hrs	min
Name of Show										
Time On	:		:		:		:		:	
Time Off	:		:		:		:		:	
Time Watched	hrs	min	hrs	min	hrs	min	hrs	min	hrs	min
Name of Show										
Time On	:		:		:		:		:	
Time Off	:		:		:		:		:	
Time Watched	hrs	min	hrs	min	hrs	min	hrs	min	hrs	min
Name of Show										
Time On	:		:		:		:		:	
Time Off	:		:		:		:		:	
Time Watched	hrs	min	hrs	min	hrs	min	hrs	min	hrs	min
Name of Show										
Time On	:		:		:		:		:	
Time Off	:		:		:		:		:	
Time Watched	hrs	min	hrs	min	hrs	min	hrs	min	hrs	min
Name of Show										
Total Daily Time	hrs	min	hrs	min	hrs	min	hrs	min	hrs	min

TV TIME SLIPS

(Photocopy as many as you need and place by every television set)

Name _____

Date _____

Time On _____ Time Off _____

Time Watched _____ hrs _____ min _____

Name of Show _____

--- --- --- --- --- --- --- --- --- --- --- --- --- --- --- ✄

Name _____

Date _____

Time On _____ Time Off _____

Time Watched _____ hrs _____ min _____

Name of Show _____

--- --- --- --- --- --- --- --- --- --- --- --- --- --- --- ✄

Name _____

Date _____

Time On _____ Time Off _____

Time Watched _____ hrs _____ min _____

Name of Show _____

--- --- --- --- --- --- --- --- --- --- --- --- --- --- --- ✄

Name _____

Date _____

Time On _____ Time Off _____

Time Watched _____ hrs _____ min _____

Name of Show _____

--- --- --- --- --- --- --- --- --- --- --- --- --- --- --- ✄

Complete this worksheet for each program identified by your station as "specifically designed to meet the educational and informational needs of children" or other programming that helps to meet the requirements of the Children's Television Act.

Name of Program: _____

SECTION 1: Information From the Public Inspection File

Give the program description as contained in the Public Inspection File:

Is it targeted to specific groups?   What age?

Note any other comments made in the file about this program.

SECTION 2: Scoring the Program

For each criterion, rate the program according to the scale below. When you are finished, add up the numbers in the right-hand column to get a "quality score" out of a possible 30 points.

This Program . . .

1	Speaks to children in ways they can understand.	1	2	3
2	Includes educational content, such as news, history, geography, biography, math or science.	1	2	3
3	Encourages children to think about their feelings, learn about the world, and increase their self-worth.	1	2	3
4	Shows gender differences fairly; boys and girls are shown as being able to do the same things and have the same goals.	1	2	3
5	Presents racial and ethnic groups positively. Does not reinforce stereotypes.	1	2	3
6	Deals with conflict constructively and presents it in a way children can understand.	1	2	3
7	Is appropriate for its targeted age group.	1	2	3
8	Is paced to allow children to think about and absorb its content.	1	2	3
9	Simulates constructive activities that may enhance the quality of a child's play.	1	2	3
10	Compares favorably with other children's programs you have seen.	1	2	3

Total Points _____ **/ 30**

The Media
Consumer's
Resource Guide

A. Watchdog and Advocacy Groups

The Center for Media Education (CME)
1511 K Street, NW, Suite 518
Washington, DC 20005
Tel.: 202-628-2620
Fax: 202-628-2554

The Center for Media Education was founded in 1991 to promote the democratic potential of the electronic media. The center organizes and educates consumer groups and nonprofit organizations on issues of public policy and the media, and will provide referrals and technical support. It also serves as a clearinghouse for reporters and editors; researches and analyzes trends in electronic media; and prepares FCC and FTC filings on behalf of nonprofit organizations.

PROJECTS:
Campaign for Kids' TV. Aimed at improving the quality of children's television.

Future of Media Project. Dedicated to fostering a public interest vision for the new media and information superhighway of the twenty-first century.

Unplug
360 Grand Avenue
Box 385
Oakland, CA 94610
Tel.: 800-UNPLUG1 or 510-268-1100
Fax: 510-268-1277

A national nonprofit youth organization dedicated to creating commercial-free and equal education that is community, rather than corporate, controlled. Founded to serve as a vehicle for youth opposition to Channel One, and to link students to parent-teacher and community organizations, UNPLUG produces educational materials about media literacy and educational equality. It also provides direct assistance to students through workshops and training, and serves as a clearinghouse for information about commercialism and other issues that concern youth.

PUBLICATIONS:
Quarterly Newspaper. Covers national social issues that concern youth today.

ORGANIZING KITS:
Step-by-step instructions that students can take to "unplug commercialism from the school."

VIDEOTAPES:
Commercial Free Zone. Brief video encouraging students to question messages from advertisements on Channel One (free to students).

B. Selected Media Literacy Organizations

Center for Media Literacy
1962 S. Shenandoah
Los Angeles, CA 90034
Tel.: 310-559-2944
Fax: 310-559-9396

The Center for Media Literacy (formerly the Center for Media and Values) is a nonprofit membership organization established to translate media literacy research, analysis, theory, and practice into information, training, and practical educational tools for teachers, educators, parents, and caregivers of children. As advocates, resource providers, and educators, members of the center encourage accountability and responsibility of both media producers and their audiences, and cooperate with the leaders of the worldwide media-literacy movement to stimulate advances in the field. Memberships begin at $35 per year, and benefits include a subscription to the center's quarterly magazine, access to the helpline and information network, and discounts on publications and teaching resources.

PUBLICATIONS:
Media & Values magazine (quarterly) covers media trends and current developments in television, mass media, and popular culture. Includes practical ideas for media literacy in the classroom, the community, and the home, as well as reviews, commentary, and opinion.

The center's Media Literacy Workshop Kits are thematic curriculum units with step-by-step Leader's Guides to use for youth and adult groups in schools, churches, after-school programs, and community centers. Each kit includes an illustrated series including handout masters (with reprint permission), and some kits contain video components. Popular titles include: *Break the Lies That Bind* (sexism in the media); *News for the '90s* (how to watch the news); *Parenting in a TV Age* (a parent education course); *Images of Conflict: Learning from Media Coverage of the Gulf War; Selling Addiction* (combating tobacco and alcohol advertising); *Living in the Image Culture: A Media Literacy Primer; Citizenship in a Media Age* (media and the political process); *TV Alert: A Wake-Up Guide to Television Literacy; Global Questions: Exploring World Media Issues;* and *Beyond Blame: Countering Violence in the Media.* (Prices range from $21.95 to $99.95 plus shipping.)

The Children's Television Resource and Education Center (C-TREC)
340 Townsend Street
San Francisco, CA 94107
Tel.: 415-243-9943
Fax: 415-243-9037

C-TREC is a nonprofit educational corporation dedicated to creating services and products that promote children's social development and academic success, and helping parents, teachers, and other professionals deal with issues related to children and television. The center offers media literacy presentations, media consultation services, and education and entertainment products for the print, audio, video, and computer software markets that enhance children's social development.

PUBLICATIONS:
TV Breakouts: Guides to help parents cope with television, video games, and music videos. Single copies available for free in English and Spanish (nominal charge for bulk orders).

PRESENTATIONS:
Helping Children Survive Television. Conducted by the center's Television Awareness Training Institute.

AUDIOCASSETTES AND BOOKS:

GETTING ALONG Stories and Songs. Songs, stories, and activities to help kids work and play together ($12.95 plus shipping). Contact JTG of Nashville, 800-222-2584.

The Adventures of Christina Valentine. A dramatic audio series about a young teenager who looks to television for solutions to her real-life problems ($15.95 plus tax where appropriate and $2.00 shipping).

EDUCATIONAL PRODUCTS:

GETTING ALONG: A Social Development Curriculum (K-4). A curriculum for helping children develop skills in cooperation, caring for others, critical thinking, and positive conflict resolution. Contains a teacher's guide and other materials. (Contact AGS, Inc., 800-328-2560.)

OTHER PRODUCTS:

TV Minder: C-TREC's "television time manager for families." Attach this six-by-eight-inch plastic clock face to the TV screen and adjust the hands to the time when TV may be turned on. A space is also provided for writing in non-TV activities with a washable, nontoxic marker. TV Minder is designed to give children a sense of responsibility and control over their viewing.

Citizens for Media Literacy
34 Wall Street, Suite 407
Asheville, NC 28801
Tel.: 704-255-0182
Fax: 704-254-2286

Citizens for Media Literacy is a nonprofit public-interest organization that links media literacy with the concepts and practices of citizenship. Activities include lobbying for media literacy in schools and in the home, promoting citizens' responsibility for free speech rights, assisting citizen activists and journalists on issues related to the Freedom of Information Act and Open Records laws, encouraging public access to the media (especially via cable), gaining access to the information superhighway, and publishing media analyses and criticism. CML sponsors conferences and symposia, publishes a newsletter (available by subscription at $15 per year), and distributes bumper stickers and posters.

PUBLICATIONS:
The New Citizen. A quarterly newsletter that covers media literacy and TV-viewing skills, media advertising and violence, free speech advocacy, etc.
Get a Life! An instructional comic book designed to help teenagers resist the influence of TV advertising.
Reprints: Commentaries and article reprints on media literacy topics (slight charge for production and postage).

AUDIOTAPES:
Lecture series audiotapes include: *Re-Thinking Democracy: Citizenship in the Age of Mass Media; Down the Tubes: TV's Threat to Democracy; Whose First Amendment Is It, Anyway?;* and *The Age of Missing Information.*

Institute for Mental Health Initiatives
4545 42nd Street, NW
Suite 311
Washington, DC 20016
Tel.: 202-364-7111
Fax: 202-363-3891

The institute is a nonprofit organization dedicated to promoting mental health and preventing emotional disorders. It translates research from the mental health community into programs, products, and information that is accessible to the public. The institute also encourages writers, producers, and directors to include in their story lines issues relating to conflict resolution and anger management skills and to provide more positive models of human interaction.

PUBLICATIONS:
Various pamphlets for parents on how to manage anger and deal with TV violence (free of charge—call or write).

VIDEOTAPES:
Anger Management for Parents. (Distributed through Research Press, 217-352-3273; $200, rentals available at $55 for three days, free preview.)

MEDIA WATCH

P.O. Box 618
Santa Cruz, CA 95061-0618
Tel.: 408-423-6355

Media Watch is a nonprofit organization dedicated to improving the image of women in the media, educating individuals concerning the consequences of sexually objectifying women and children in the media, and helping people become more critical consumers of all forms of mass media.

PUBLICATIONS:
Action Agenda. A quarterly newsletter covering a variety of issues related to television, radio, and other mass media ($10 to $20, sliding scale).

VIDEOTAPES:
Warning: The Media May Be Hazardous to Your Health and *Don't Be a TV-Television Victim* (helps viewers think about TV's portrayal of violence, sensationalism, and stereotypes).
(Price: $150 for institutions, $40 for individuals, plus $5 shipping. Previews and rentals available. Instructor's Guides to both videos are available for $7 to $10, sliding scale.)

National Telemedia Council, Inc.

120 East Wilson Street
Madison, WI 53703
Tel.: 608-257-7712
Fax: 608-257-7714

The National Telemedia Council assists educators in developing practical approaches to teaching media literacy. A new initiative of NTC, the Media Literacy Clearinghouse and Center, provides customized references and resources for the teaching of media literacy, as well as notices of upcoming national conferences and workshops, annotated bibliographies and directories related to media literacy, and teacher-support materials for integrating media literacy concepts into the classroom. The basic individual membership is $30. Contact the organization for information about school and corporate memberships. Members receive *Telemedium* and *Telemedium Update* (see below), as well as discounts on conference registration fees and printed materials.

PUBLICATIONS:
Telemedium. A quarterly publication featuring thought-provoking articles written by media literacy leaders, book reviews, and classroom/home teaching activities.

Telemedium Update. A bulletin that keeps readers in touch with NTC's activities.

Strategies for Media Literacy, Inc.
1095 Market Street, Suite 617
San Francisco, CA 94103
Tel.: 415-621-2911

Strategies for Media Literacy, Inc., is a national nonprofit organization that promotes media literacy beginning in early elementary education. The organization develops and publishes materials, identifies resources, conducts media literacy workshops, provides consulting services, and serves as a center of support and contact for teachers of media in the United States.

PUBLICATIONS:
Strategies. A quarterly newsletter that contains media literacy news from around the world, profiles of media educators, and resources to teach about media ($15 per year for individuals, $30 per year for organizations).

EDUCATIONAL PRODUCTS:
Media & You: An Elementary Media Literacy Curriculum. An activity book with strategies for teaching students to think critically about media ($29.95).

The Critical Eye: Inside TV Advertising. An interactive videodisc for the Macintosh with Hypercard 2.1 about advertising, designed for the secondary classroom and for staff development ($89.95).

WORKSHOPS:
Conducts media-literacy training workshops throughout the country at various school districts.

BBS: 415-621-5156
The Media Literacy BBS is an electronic bulletin board that provides information on current media education news and events.

C. Research Organizations

The Center for Research on the Influences of Television on Children (CRITC)
Department of Human Development
University of Kansas
4084 Dole Hall
Lawrence, KS 66045
Tel.: 913-864-4646

CRITC is devoted to studying how children interact with television. It is particularly concerned with home-viewing patterns of young children, the way children distinguish between fiction and reality, and the use of instructional television to present science and math concepts. Research reports are available in the form of reprints.

Mediascope
12711 Ventura Blvd.
Suite 250
Studio City, CA 91604
Tel.: 818-508-2080
Fax: 818-508-2088

Mediascope is a nonprofit public-interest organization that promotes the constructive depiction of social and health issues in the media. Funded primarily through grants, the organization focuses heavily on the education of the entertainment industry about the relationship between on-screen violence and aggression in society. In addition to sponsoring informational forums on various topics, Mediascope provides story and script consultation, initiates original research, and serves as a clearinghouse on research, public policy, and social issues related to the media.

PUBLICATIONS:
Transcripts of forums, fact sheets, research studies, and research bibliographies (geared for research and media professionals). Contact Mediascope for pricing information.

VIDEOTAPES:
The Kids Are Watching. A 13-minute 1/2-inch VHS tape on children's reactions and opinions to media violence. $12.00, including shipping.

Yale University Family Television Research and Consultation Center

Department of Psychology
P.O. Box 208205
New Haven, CT 06520-8205
Tel.: 203-432-4565
Fax: 203-432-7172

The Yale University Family Television Research and Consultation Center focuses on the role of television and other forms of communication in child/adolescent development and lifestyle. The center evaluates children's programming, helps parents and educators limit television watching, and offers advice on using the media to enhance children's cognitive, social, emotional, and physical development. Additionally, the center provides communication- and television-related books, journals, government reports, and other resources to students, faculty, and other professionals. The center also conducts Parent Workshops on television; publishes findings in magazine articles, books, and professional journals; and provides speakers to organizations and the media.

D. Organizations that Deal with Advertising and Consumerism

Adbusters Media Foundation

1243 West 7th Avenue
Vancouver, BC V6H 1B7
Tel.: 800-663-1243 or 604-736-9401
Fax: 604-737-6021

The foundation is a magazine publisher and video producer, as well as a nonprofit advertising agency that creates ad campaigns for Greenpeace, Friends of Clayquot Sound, and other environmental organizations.

PUBLICATIONS:
Adbusters Quarterly: The Journal of the Mental Environment. Explores the billion-dollar advertising industry and how it affects our culture. (Individual rate: four issues for $18.00, eight issues for $30. Higher institutional rate. Some back issues available. Individual copies: $5.75.)

Adbusters offers a number of "uncommercials" or "culture-jamming TV-spots" designed to jolt viewers into thinking about major issues of our day. Available on VHS format for $25.00 each; broadcast-quality copies are available free of charge for use on community television or for paid time on your local commercial station.

The Center for the Study of Commercialism
1875 Connecticut Avenue, NW
Suite 300
Washington, DC 20009
Tel.: 202-332-9110
Fax: 202-265-4954

A nonprofit, membership-based organization concerned with the harmful effects of excessive commercialism in our society. The use of television to promote commercialism and the growing ubiquity of television are key areas of study. In addition to its quarterly newsletter, *Advice,* the center has published a primer on advertising titled *Dictating Content.* The directors of the center also authored *Marketing Madness* (Westview Press, 1994). Individuals can join for $20 per year, and members receive the center's quarterly newsletter, as well as discounts on all center publications.

PUBLICATIONS:
Dictating Content: How Advertising Pressure Can Corrupt a Free Press ($10.00).
Advice. Quarterly newsletter covering problematic advertising and marketing practices in the U.S. and abroad.

E. Recommended Books and Videotapes

Books:
Bennett, Steve, and Ruth Bennett. *365 TV-Free Activities You Can Do with Your Child.* Bob Adams, Inc. 1991
Bennett, Steve, and Ruth Bennett. *365 OUTDOOR Activities You Can Do with Your Child.* Bob Adams, Inc. 1991
Carlsson-Paige, Nancy, and Diane E. Levin. *Who's Calling the Shots? How to Respond Effectively to Children's Fascination with War Play and War Toys.* New Society Publishers, 1990.

Considine, David, and Gail Haley. *Visual Messages: Integrating Imagery into Instruction.* Library Unlimited, 1992.

Houston, Aletha, et al. *Big World, Small Screen: The Role of Television in American Society.* University of Nebraska Press, 1992.

Imber-Black, Evan, and Janine Roberts. *Rituals for Our Times: Celebrating, Healing, and Changing Our Lives and Our Relationships.* HarperCollins, 1993.

Levin, Diane E. *Teaching Young Children in Violent Times: Building a Peaceable Classroom.* Cambridge Educators for Social Responsibility, 1994.

McKibben, Bill. *The Age of Missing Information.* Plume, 1993.

Mitroff, Ian, and Warren Bennis. *The Unreality Industry: The Deliberate Manufacturing of Falsehood and What It Is Doing to Our Lives.* Oxford University Press, 1989.

Postman, Neil. *Amusing Ourselves to Death: Public Discourse in the Age of Show Business.* Penguin, 1985.

Prochaska, James, John Norcross, and Carlo DiClemente. *Changing for Good.* Morrow, 1994.

Singer, Dorthy G., Jerome L. Singer, and Diana M. Zuckerman. *Use TV to Your Child's Advantage.* Acropolis Books, Ltd., 1990.

Videotapes:

Teach the Children: The New Video on Kids & TV. This fifty-eight-minute video chronicles the continuing tensions in telecommunication policy between public service and private gain—from the Communications Act of 1934 to the Children's Television Act of 1990. It explores how the U.S. is virtually the only country in the world to allow commercial interests almost unfettered access to our children's minds. Price is $49 plus $5 shipping.

Resolution, Inc./California Newsreel
149 Ninth Street, #420
San Francisco, CA 94103
Tel: 415-621-6196

F. TV Lockout/Control Devices

SuperVision
This electronic device can be programmed to limit TV viewing to specific schedules and to daily and weekly viewing allowances. It can also track how much TV each child views. $99.99.

Tectrics Labs, Inc.
5256 South Mission Road
Suite 110
Bonsall, CA 92003
800-845-1911
619-631-3080

The Switch
The Switch is a mechanical device that regulates the flow of electricity to the TV with a key. The TV's plug is encased in a childproof compartment so children can't reconnect the set. $21.95 plus $3.50 shipping.

The Switch
267 Walker Avenue
Clarendon Hills, IL 60514
800-535-5845

Time Slot
This electronic device allows parents to regulate the TV viewing of up to eight children. They can allocate specific viewing allowances for each child, and fully block certain viewing times. The unit includes an audit feature, and relies on magnetic "credit cards" for use and programming. $99.99

Design Dimension, Inc.
901 North West Street
Raleigh, NC 27603
919-828-1485

TV Allowance
This television control device can be used to regulate the viewing habits of up to four children. Parents can allocate a weekly viewing

allowance and block out up to three time periods. A programmable feature allows children to accumulate their allowance from week to week. The unit is activated by unique four-digit codes entered on a keypad. $99.

TV Allowance
5605 SW 74th Street, #21
South Miami, FL 33143
800-231-4410

FOR THE BEST IN PAPERBACKS, LOOK FOR THE

In every corner of the world, on every subject under the sun, Penguin represents quality and variety—the very best in publishing today.

For complete information about books available from Penguin—including Pelicans, Puffins, Peregrines, and Penguin Classics—and how to order them, write to us at the appropriate address below. Please note that for copyright reasons the selection of books varies from country to country.

In the United Kingdom: For a complete list of books available from Penguin in the U.K., please write to *Dept E.P., Penguin Books Ltd, Harmondsworth, Middlesex, UB7 0DA.*

In the United States: For a complete list of books available from Penguin in the U.S., please write to *Consumer Sales, Penguin USA, P.O. Box 999—Dept. 17109, Bergenfield, New Jersey 07621-0120.* VISA and MasterCard holders call 1-800-253-6476 to order all Penguin titles.

In Canada: For a complete list of books available from Penguin in Canada, please write to *Penguin Books Canada Ltd, 10 Alcorn Avenue, Suite 300, Toronto, Ontario, Canada M4V 3B2.*

In Australia: For a complete list of books available from Penguin in Australia, please write to the *Marketing Department, Penguin Books Ltd, P.O. Box 257, Ringwood, Victoria 3134.*

In New Zealand: For a complete list of books available from Penguin in New Zealand, please write to the *Marketing Department, Penguin Books (NZ) Ltd, Private Bag, Takapuna, Auckland 9.*

In India: For a complete list of books available from Penguin, please write to *Penguin Overseas Ltd, 706 Eros Apartments, 56 Nehru Place, New Delhi, 110019.*

In Holland: For a complete list of books available from Penguin in Holland, please write to *Penguin Books Nederland B.V., Postbus 195, NL-1380AD Weesp, Netherlands.*

In Germany: For a complete list of books available from Penguin, please write to *Penguin Books Ltd, Friedrichstrasse 10-12, D-6000 Frankfurt Main 1, Federal Republic of Germany.*

In Spain: For a complete list of books available from Penguin in Spain, please write to *Longman, Penguin España, Calle San Nicolas 15, E-28013 Madrid, Spain.*

In Japan: For a complete list of books available from Penguin in Japan, please write to *Longman Penguin Japan Co Ltd, Yamaguchi Building, 2-12-9 Kanda Jimbocho, Chiyoda-Ku, Tokyo 101, Japan.*

FOR THE BEST IN PAPERBACKS, LOOK FOR THE

☐ **READ ALL ABOUT IT!**
Great Read-Aloud Stories, Poems, and Newspaper Pieces for Preteens to Teens
Jim Trelease

Trelease turns his attention to older children with a read-aloud collection of forty-eight wide-ranging and culturally diverse selections from newspapers, magazines, and books, aimed at the special interests of adolescents. *512 pages* *ISBN: 0-14-014655-5*

☐ **CABIN FEVER**
202 Activities for Turning Your Child's Rainy Days, Snow Days, and Sick Days into Great Days
Steve and Ruth Bennett

Relieve the boredom and restlessness of days spent indoors! Uniquely tailored to parents and caregivers, *Cabin Fever* is teeming with easy, creative, educational activities which will provide endless hours of stimulating, lively entertainment.
240 pages *ISBN: 0-14-023909-X*

☐ **THE NEW READ-ALOUD HANDBOOK**
Jim Trelease

Help children become lifetime readers! This giant treasury of read-aloud books will help parents, teachers, grandparents, siblings, and librarians start children on the road to improving their language skills and awakening their imaginations.
320 pages *ISBN: 0-14-046881-1*

☐ **GOOD NEWS**
How Sharing the Newspaper with Your Children Can Enhance Their Performance in School
Deborah Drezon Carroll

Headlines and op-ed pages, the TV schedule and the comics—every section of the newspaper can help children develop reading and learning skills, as well as foster a lifelong interest in the world and its happenings. *144 pages* *ISBN: 0-14-017039-1*